John Anakwenze

The Bee Chase

novum ⬗ pro

This book is also available as e-book.

www.novum-publishing.co.uk

© 2018 novum publishing

All rights of distribution, including via film, radio, and television, photomechanical reproduction, audio storage media, electronic data storage media, and the reprinting of portions of text, are reserved.

Printed in the European Union on environmentally friendly, chlorine- and acid-free paper.

ISBN 978-3-99064-243-6
Editing: novum publishing
Cover photo:
Lane Erickson | Dreamstime.com
Cover design, layout & typesetting:
novum publishing
Internal illustration:
Candaxyatul | Dreamstime.com

www.novum-publishing.co.uk

Chapter One

Udenka was only four-years-old, small for his age, thin with short arms and a long neck. He was so thin that his siblings always told him he could easily be blown away by the wind. He had a well-shaped, handsome face. He walked delicately, hardly swinging his arms, as if he was going to trip over and fall at any moment. He appeared frail and had developed a habit of walking bent over, looking down to avoid making eye contact with adults coming in the opposite direction, as he was extremely shy. He already knew what the word "disappointment" meant because admission to primary school was nearly beyond his reach. He had tried for two years to be accepted by the head teacher. Admission to the primary school was done once a year. Each time he was turned down, not because he had failed any written entrance examination, for there was none; it was more of a physical examination. The first time Udenka went to meet the head teacher to be assessed for admission early one morning, the teacher unceremoniously swung his right arm violently across the top of his head to touch the opposite ear, but, to his disappointment, his fingers could not reach it. He was summarily dismissed in the most impolite way, which a child could not comprehend.

It was a dreaded sentence of one long year at home while his peers were in school. Udenka's small size had failed him. His growth was static as he ate poorly because of constant ill health. He often turned away and rejected most of the cooked meals his parents could afford. His parents were not well off and struggled to make ends meet. His mother, Udego, found it most frustrating and had to resort to forced feeding as a means of solving this persistent problem. She eventually became so experienced in this that she could be regarded as an expert. Udego would easily put this small figure across her lap with a cup full of semi-liquid food perched in one hand, deftly closing his nostrils with her free hand, and while he screamed and gasped, she simultaneously put the food in his mouth to coincide with his intake of breath. It was generally felt that there was no way he would live to adulthood if no action were taken, hence Udego resorted to this extreme measure.

Other contributing factors to Udenka's diminutive figure included irregular and late meals. Unfortunately for a growing child, supper was always very late at night. Udego was very busy during the day and would start cooking late in the evening. It could be six o'clock in the evening before she would decide what to cook and only then would she begin to gather ingredients for making soup. At that point, it would occur to her that firewood needed to be collected to make a fire. Someone was then sent to the nearby forest to gather wood. This process of gathering wood and making a fire would take in the region of one hour, much longer if the wood was wet, as often happened during the rainy season. With the pot on the freshly made fire outside, as there was no kitchen enclosure as such, the items needed to make the soup were added methodically at various stages of the cooking process. This resulted in the cooking taking much longer. Each item was put in the cooking pot at least thirty minutes apart from each other. A completely well-cooked soup containing a full complement of ingredients took an average of four hours. You could hear the pounding of food in the dead of night when most of the villagers were already fast asleep. While the children waited anxiously for the food to be ready, Udenka would by now have fallen asleep on the rough floor, awoken a few times to the loud pounding of yams.

With the food now ready, his problem was not yet solved, for the actual eating of the food was as complex a problem as the cooking and needed determination, resourcefulness and wisdom. The older ones fared better. To begin with, there was poor lighting because the entire family ate at night in the large sitting room that was sparsely furnished, and there was only one functioning lamp that was never bright enough. His parents ate together and all the siblings gathered round a plate of soup containing fish and pieces of meat and another plate of pounded yam. To survive, you must eat fast, and the older siblings were better at it, tending to eat faster than the younger ones. The entire meal disappeared in a matter of minutes. To make the dire situation worse for the younger siblings, the parents would always send one of them on an errand that required the use of the only lamp at the most critical point of the eating process. With one child called away to fetch something unimportant, the rest would continue to eat in darkness, unnoticed. One older mischievous sibling would shift the soup plate from its normal position in the dark. Udenka, not knowing the soup bowl had been shifted from the usual position, would dip the pounded yam bolus into what he thought was the soup plate but inadvertently dipped it on the floor. When the lamp was eventually brought back, the plates were found to be empty, as the rest of the meal had been consumed in darkness. Udenka was worse off at supper, even though he was awake, as he was unable to compete with his older siblings. He was also disadvantaged in other ways. The pieces of meat and dry fish in the soup plate were the only sources of protein, and these were normally left until the end of the meal, to be shared equally among the siblings. Unfortunately, at the end of such a meal, there was not much to share because as they ate fast the pieces would be cleverly wedged unseen between the bolus and swallowed by the older siblings. The younger ones had no chance. They were too young to compete with the dexterity of their older siblings.

Twelve months of doing nothing in the remote village was hell for him. He was left at home most days with his younger sister, who was only two years old at that time, as his companion. Udego would leave early in the morning for the market several miles away and was not expected back until late in the evening. His father, Fidelis, was always out teaching in a school as a head teacher. Both were therefore left at home for several hours to fend for themselves. They would try to see who cried the loudest and longest for most of the day in expectation of their parents' return. He seemed to blame his parents for the situation he found himself in, and he resorted to mischievous behaviour. One day, while playing outside, a very aggressive hen herding ten-day-old chicks started picking with its beak at a fresh wound on his shin covered with cotton wool. He continued chasing the hen away only for it to come back when he was inattentive, picking at the dressed wound until it started to bleed profusely. With his parents away, he decided on immediate action and he didn't have time to consider the consequences. He chased the hen, caught up with it, and strangled it. He took the dead hen into the back garden, dug a shallow grave and buried it. He forgot his wicked action until his mum came back from the market to find the young chickens running aimlessly up and down the compound. His mum, Udego, began to ask about the hen that was supposed to care for and protect the young chicks. In no time, she began to suspect an elderly neighbour who lived alone and who was once caught late at night stealing their livestock. The matter did not develop further and he felt relieved. His mum directed all her anger towards her neighbour, and he felt his dastardly action would go undetected and gave it no further thought.

Months later, one early morning, he woke up to the sound of footsteps that he thought, as always, came from his mum, about to leave for the far away market. He dreaded it. The entire time was spent roaming about the huge compound unsupervised. Late that sunny afternoon, everything appeared calm and eerily quiet. The villagers went about their normal business. The young ones were out in the morning for the farm, leaving the elderly at home, and were noticeable as they cut across the mission.

Suddenly, there seemed to be a disturbance among the livestock including goats and cows because they became restless and started making peculiar, distressed noises. Then, in a blink of an eye, they started to run across the yard as if in a panic. When he looked up to the sky, it appeared as if the moon was fighting the sun. Men rushed out of their homes and tried to escape with their goats perched around their necks, cock in one hand, as they started to run. As their speed quickened, Udenka could hear them talking about the end of the world. He could see the villagers move in different directions. Darkness inexplicably descended on the village, taking over the normally bright, cloudless, sunny afternoon. It now seemed to him as he looked towards the sky that the world was truly suddenly coming to an end. To reinforce what he had seen, the normally placid villagers rushed out of their compounds carrying whatever they could lay their hands on at such short notice, heading nowhere in particular. What he was witnessing was too much for a four-year-old boy. At that point, he got frightened and quickly grabbed his younger sister, already crying her eyes out, in one hand, and dashed across the compound where they found themselves in the middle of a dusty but lonely road, which rarely welcomed one vehicle in an entire month. At that same moment, an army jeep painted in brown with a flag hoisted on the bonnet was approaching fast and was forced to make a sudden, unscheduled stop with brakes screeching and smoke rising from its tyres, mixed with the rising dust, to avoid running them over.

It was around the time of the Second World War. Two young men in army uniform jumped out of the vehicle, grabbed the two children, and moved them to safety.

While this was happening, in no time, a crowd of panicked villagers who had initially bolted had surrounded the vehicle and were looking at the two white men, with their goats still perched on their necks. The villagers looked anxious with eyes bulging and lips moving nervously as if asking for an explanation for the events just witnessed. This time, the darkness had lifted and sunshine once again lit up the village. The white men noticed the stark terror in the eyes of the villagers and tried to calm them down by explaining in English exactly what had happened. Unfortunately, the villagers were pagans and had no formal education. All the same, they listened attentively, unsure of what was being said. Udenka could pick out a few English words, for he was taught at home by his father. From what he could gather, they were reassuring the villagers that it was not the end of the world but a natural phenomenon – a total solar eclipse of the sun. At the end of the lecture, the villagers, in their ignorance, turned their backs and walked off. They couldn't be bothered. They needed no explanation. They could now see it. With the darkness lifted, it was not the end of the world after all.

Chapter Two

The following year, the admission process was repeated. The night before, Udenka hardly slept. He dreaded another year at home. At that age, there was no way to know how to strengthen his arms in such a way as to pass the test. He had insignificant growth the whole of that year and he once more failed the test. At that point, he felt he would never go to school. He walked back home dejected and sad, crying all the way. It again meant another one year idling at home. His peers had now been in school for one uninterrupted year.

He lived with his parents in a mission covering a large expanse of well-kept land surrounded by thick hedges. Despite its size, it contained a building standing alone in the middle of this well-kept compound. The rest of the villagers lived not far apart from the mission and they revered, respected and adored Udenka's family. Education was in its infancy. The villagers were absorbed in their primitive ways of life and young girls and women were scantily dressed. He often stood there watching villagers pass through the mission on their way to the market.

The daily routine was monotonous. He was woken up along with his siblings at first crow around four in the morning, and quickly got ready to fetch water some distance away. With empty clay pots balanced on their heads, they were off on foot to the stream, four miles away. The route was frighteningly quiet and lonely. Not a sound could be heard. Along the way, they said little as it was too early in the morning, and they were afraid of being heard by evil spirits lurking in the dark. The silence of the night was disarming and instilled fear in all of them as they progressed towards the stream. As they got closer and the stream became visible, the leader of their group would start shouting at the top of his or her voice, invoking evil spirits to leave the stream so they could be allowed to bathe and fetch water. Having bathed and with the clay pots full of water well positioned on their heads, they made their way back home. It so often happened that with the heavy load on Udenka's head becoming unbearable and his long neck beginning to shrink, he would start grunting in pain and soon after dislodged the clay pot from his head, smashing it on the hard surface. Now that his head was free from any luggage, he would cry all the way home, holding on to small pieces of the broken pot to be blamed and at the same time consoled by his caring, sympathetic mum. No matter what length his mum took in reducing the size of the clay pot, the outcome was the same: every pot was smashed on his way home from the stream. He eventually ended up accompanying his siblings to the stream without a clay pot, while his mum counted the cost of broken pots.

His father, Fidelis, broke the monotony of village life by inviting the villagers once in a long while to listen to gramophone records at night. On the appointed day, it seemed that the entire village began to arrive until the front of the mission house was packed full. His dad would then start playing the first record. He always played the "Laughing Scotsman" first. They waited anxiously, whispering to one another, not knowing what music would come on. When the "Laughing Scotsman" record came on, it suddenly brought about endless laughter and merriment. You could see them peeping into the gramophone, trying to get a glimpse of whoever was making the sound they were listening to. It was the first time some of the villagers were seeing a gramophone; Fidelis was the only one in the village who owned such a thing. They stayed far into the night listening to various records before eventually retiring, feeling on top of the world, for night well spent. To the villagers, such kind gestures would remain a topic of conversation, punctuating their boring, repetitive, never-ending tasks essential for survival.

It was on the third attempt that Udenka was accepted into his first school. He realised that his peers had been in school for two years running while he was stuck at home. He was determined to work hard to recover lost time and wrongly assumed that with more effort, he would catch up with his age mates. He was so excited at starting school that he waited in eager anticipation; the night before school resumed, he hardly slept and hardly ate his supper. More importantly, he sat down with his older brother, already in the same school, and bombarded him with questions about what school life was like. He heard nothing to encourage him but tale of dirty and dangerous pranks in the class during lessons and the constant floggings by teachers. He told Udenka what happened one morning in class while he listened attentively to a lesson, with his eyes fixed on the teacher writing on the blackboard with white chalk. One mischievous boy next to him put a matchbox full of deadly scorpions in his side pocket. His brother never realised something was in his side pocket until he was stung by a black scorpion that had crawled out of the matchbox. Udenka was so moved by these stories that he was full of fear and anticipation as his mum took him to his class.

Nothing untoward took place on his first day at school. He began to settle down to schoolwork and the routine. He started to make friends in earnest. The first boy he picked in his class lived close to the mission and had previously met him on a few occasions. His name was Ndu. Udenka chose him out of sympathy for him because of his home circumstances. He was the same age as Udenka. Ndu's mother was long dead. He lived with his dad in a clearing in the bush without a single structure. There was no food or cooking utensils for one to talk of cooked meals. What he had for a father was a tall pagan, Ekwensu, who most of the time was seen talking to himself and related poorly to his only child. He dressed shabbily, half-naked, always wearing dirty and tattered dresses, and neighbours generally avoided him. What was most striking about this man was that half of his jaw on one side had disappeared, leaving a gaping hole from where there was a constant drooling of saliva. He was so unsightly that Udenka and other children bolted as he approached. The children could not work out how half of his jaw had been eaten away.

The man with no jaw was a typical pagan who went about offering rituals and scattering idols in the town, to the disapproval of a new Irish parish priest. They confronted each other one evening in the open and the meeting was bad tempered. Udenka watched from a distance but saw everything. They were shouting at each other while a few people gathered around them. The priest was screaming angrily in English, but Ekwensu had no basic education and was responding equally in his native dialect. The jawless man stood his ground and the Irish priest was gesticulating and shouting, pointing his fingers at him. The priest finally told him he would bring the wrath of God upon him. Ekwensu dared him to do this. The two finally parted and the reprimands did not stop Ekwensu from continuing his pagan practice.

Udenka was able to make more friends and everyone rallied round to help provide food and clothing for Ndu. Their relationship to Ndu was based on a good understanding of his home situation and on love. They had so much sympathy for him that they did their best for him, at times resorting to stealing food to make sure Ndu was comfortable. It became an obsession that carried on until they left school.

Chapter Three

Udego was hard-working and did all sorts to support her husband's meagre income. Now that Udenka was in school, his mum felt he was old enough to start selling items for her. He was smart and pleasant. Villagers easily warmed up to him and would readily buy from him rather than from someone else. He was so well loved by the villagers. His mum would wake up in the early hours of the morning to fry akara to be sold rather than for household consumption. He would carry a whole basin full of hot akara to sell to villagers before going to school, a feat he had mastered well – he had done it so often. He would then come back and quickly dress up for school. He was never late for lectures apart from one day, through no fault of his, he arrived when the lesson had already started.

The school day in question looked like any other day. The sun was out and he woke to the singing of birds, screeching of crickets and croaking of frogs. Nothing was different. It was a morning routine that he rarely sweated over. Things did not get off to a smooth start. Udego took longer than usual to get the akara ready for him. She eventually lifted the basin full of akara on to Udenka's head and he was off to trade. Within an hour, he had sold everything and the basin was empty. He wasn't sure if he had collected the correct money as he was slow at mathematics. To him, what was important when confronting his mum on return was the fact that he had sold it all and the basin was empty. He was by now running late for school. He got ready in such a rush and left the house with his schoolbag half full, as there was very little time to gather his things. To get to school he had to cover a distance of three miles along a lonely footpath that cut across thick forest. He walked fast. As he trekked gingerly along the narrow footpath, nothing in particular came to his mind. It was a lonely walk, but as he covered half the distance he came to a clearing where he saw around four schoolboys in full uniform looking up at a massive tree with a thick trunk. Udenka wondered why, when he himself was already late for lectures, the boys were loitering around a tree. He then realised they were busy throwing stones at something up in the tree. Before he could work out what was happening, as he approached the schoolchildren, heaven broke loose and he saw himself running for precious life. They had disturbed a beehive, and they were being chased by a countless angry bees who had been unnecessarily disturbed while resting in their hive peacefully.

They were stung at several points on their bodies as they ran to evade them. The boy in front of Udenka was agile, light-footed and capable of making a dash to escape this unexpected situation. Udenka knew the only way to survive was making sure he kept up with this particular fast boy in front of him. The other boys ran in different directions. He just kept going, within sight of the front runner. The boy could run. Udenka never imagined finding himself in a situation like this with his life suddenly in danger. They carried on running, still chased by the bees buzzing loudly and stinging them at the same time. They had no other choice but to continue to run, but as their legs began to tire they noticed that the school was in sight. They kept on until they ran into the school compound to their relief, but unfortunately still in the company of the chasing, relentless bees.

Finally, both ran into their classroom at full speed. As far as they could see as they approached the class, it seemed unbelievably tranquil and full of schoolchildren. The teacher was at the front, writing on the board, and the pupils were busy writing and concentrating when they suddenly ran in, sweating, panting and very panicked. A swarm of bees flew into the class with them. Everyone bolted out of the classroom, including the teacher. The bees followed them out and finally dissipated. The bees must have been equally exhausted at this point and could sting no more. When all was over, their teacher never said a word to the two latecomers who disrupted his class.

While still in school, they could hear a lot of crying, weeping and screaming coming from the nearby village, exactly like the type of sound often heard when families were bereaved. News began to come in from the village. Apparently, one of the pupils who had been involved in the bee incident was unable to escape quickly enough and had been killed by the bee stings. This made Udenka and the rest of his schoolmates sad. The sound filtering through into the school from the village would be difficult to forget. Udenka wished he would never hear such crying ever again. It touched his heart so deeply that he decided to visit the family immediately after school. As he got close to the compound, the crying became more intense and he himself started crying uncontrollably and no one could console him. The parents of the dead boy were so distraught, crying all day and throwing themselves on the ground, weeping and moving their legs about, kicking and banging their heads. Attempts to restrain them were futile. The scene Udenka witnessed was awful. The dead boy was lying on the ground, supine, and bees could be seen crawling out of his orifices, including his mouth and nose, more than ten hours after the initial attack. He was the same age as Udenka. It was a scene no young person should be allowed to witness. Udenka saw it all.

He later remembered it was not the first time he had seen a dead body nor the first heart-wrenching weeping and moaning he had ever heard. Udenka was only three years old when he had first seen a dead body. The memory started flooding in now. At the time, Udenka was unable to make head or tail of the event that overwhelmed him, but now, it began to make sense. On the day in question, he remembered going to bed as usual with his mum.

He suddenly woke up in the middle of the night only to realise he was not in bed with his mum alone, as usual – there was another woman cuddling a newborn baby lying with them. There was another lady also providing support to the lady with the baby, probably her friend. The bed became so crowded and he found himself at the bottom of the bed, almost edged out. Even though his eyes were open, he felt quite sleepy but still realised all was not well with the newborn. What struck him most was the attention being given to the child by the two women and Udenka's mum. There was so much going on in the middle of the night with the baby that the little boy had no doubt in his mind that the baby wasn't that well. How the night visitors ended up in the bedroom at that time of the night, he could not tell. They were strangers, as far as Udenka could make out. He dozed off again only to be woken up suddenly by terrible shrieking, screaming, crying and wailing, mostly from the young woman with the newborn. He could see the baby was no longer moving, crying or breathing. Udenka's mother tried to shield him from it all, but he had already seen everything he needed to see. The poor woman had suffered a terrible loss and for several months, her crying was still ringing in Udenka's ears. The question of how the woman ended up in their house in the middle of the night continued going through Udenka's mind. He picked up enough courage to ask his mother a few times for the identity of the woman with the newborn, but she wouldn't touch the topic. That night was the last time he saw the woman. She was quite young and the baby was possibly her first child, judging by how badly she took her loss. Witnessing such a loss at a young age deeply affected him. As such, he was unable to handle the bee death episode.

He was so affected and traumatised following the bee chase that he wouldn't go to school for months. His parents exhausted all means including flogging, beating to get him back to school, to no avail.

Chapter Four

Udenka's father, Fidelis, was a head teacher and therefore understood the importance of education and was pained about his child not attending classes. He did not have formal training as such to head a school. He was a tall and proud man of immense character. He was a man of contradictions, deeply religious yet still adhering to traditional values and customs. He was still a believer in herbal medicine and often invited herbalists to the house. Even at a young age, Udenka never respected herbal medicine and discredited the methods of herbalists and native doctors. His negativity was brought on by his father's belief and adherence to their practices. Fidelis suffered from poor eyesight and often brought in native doctors and herbalists to cure him. Upon the arrival of a herbalist or native doctor to the house, Udenka would watch him dig holes in the compound, after which a small mark was made close to the troubled eye of Fidelis. At the end of it all, small objects would be produced by the herbalist as coming from inside the troubled eye. Fidelis believed it came from his eye and would display the objects for all to see and he would then put them in a sealed container for preservation. Despite all of this, his sight progressively got worse, triggering more visits and more objects claimed to come from his eyes being produced by the herbalist.

Fidelis made enemies and friends in equal measure, as his job brought him in close contact with villagers away from his homeland. The villagers were mostly pagans and not keen to accept the new religion. There was so much friction. Udenka knew his dad was bold and courageous and was mostly feared. He at times had to confront the villagers in an attempt to bring more children to school. His children had occasionally observed heated exchanges but no actual fighting took place. His sons admired his courage for a very long time, but this admiration was dented by a situation that once arose at home. A large, black, dangerous snake was found in the house one sunny afternoon. Udenka was inside the house at the time. He watched his dad and mum standing in front of the hissing snake. What happened next was very unexpected. He was sure his dad, Fidelis, would go after the snake and he thought no more of it. To his surprise, Fidelis fearfully surrendered a long stick he was wielding to his wife, Udego, and expected her to deal with the snake. Traditionally, it was a man's duty to protect his wife and deal with situations like the one he found himself in. Udenka never imagined his dad would ask his mum to do this. Udego was a softly spoken, slim, beautiful, quiet woman, who now found herself in a situation where she now had to deal with a venomous snake.

She boldly took the stick and hit the snake in the head. Udenka did not know that his tender mum had that kind of courage. He felt let down by a supposedly courageous father.

Fidelis loved hunting. He had an old-style double-barrelled gun that he treasured and kept well maintained. The mission was surrounded by thick forest and every evening his dad would go into the bush to hunt. Udenka and his siblings hoped each time Fidelis went to hunt that he would come back with big game, and the children imagined and hoped to enjoy yam porridge containing bush meat from the hunting.

Each time Fidelis got back from such ventures, he would tell the children to go and retrieve an animal he shot and definitely saw falling. This happened countless times and each time, they found nothing. Being a child, Udenka was taken in because of his fondness for bush meat. Each time he was told to go and search, he immediately started salivating. He would immediately rush out to the designated forest to search the thick bush, not minding snakes and other dangerous creatures. The children were too young and too keen to obey that it did not occur to them to ask why, if their dad saw the animal fall, he could not have picked it up rather than taking the risk of his children being bitten by snakes.

Fidelis admired courageous men. There was a hunter in a village far from where they lived who killed a tiger and the news spread like uncontrollable bush fire. His father was so excited he decided to go to the distant village to pay his respect. He would not do such a thing alone, no way. He decided he would take his entire family, including the little ones. Theirs was a close-knit family and things were done together as a matter of routine. Everywhere he went, he took his family. This visit could not be an exception. It was quite a distance and needed careful preparation. The entire distance was to be covered by foot. The tiger killer knew they were coming. They took off in the morning walking at a leisurely pace with their dad in front with the little ones. They moved steadily, breaking for frequent rests when the legs of the little ones could not carry them much longer. To get to the village, they had to cross a wide stream but there was a locally improvised bridge in place and the crossing went smoothly. They eventually reached the man's house, taking them a total of four hours to get there, only to find that he was out. It was a futile venture, but they had to hurry back as it was getting late, with darkness fast approaching. They immediately headed in the direction of home. It soon started raining and it was quite a heavy downpour. They carried on despite the rain until they got to the stream, only to discover the bridge made by the natives had been washed away by the heavy rain. By now, the stream had become so swollen and the water in it fast-moving. The only way to get home was to cross the stream. There was no alternative route. Udenka was very young at the time and his younger sister two years old. The crossing was at the narrowest part of the stream but the stream proper was deep and wide. A single, rounded, smooth tree trunk was put across the gap as a makeshift bridge. It was a narrow trunk and was unsteady as you stepped on it. Fidelis carried each of the bigger children to the other end of the stream, stepping gingerly. It was still raining so the trunk was slippery, but his father was so strong, brave and full of energy. Fidelis had weighed the situation and there was no other option. It was now time for Udenka and his younger sister to be carried across. Fidelis carried them on either arm and walked slowly on the narrow, unstable trunk when suddenly his left leg slipped. Udenka looked down and could see this deep, wide stream now the size of a river. It was so big and the water was moving so fast in a wave form. Udenka saw his dad swaying and swaying on one leg and about to almost certainly fall over. Udenka knew he was looking death in the face and expected to soon drown in this normally quiet but now rain-swollen stream. He knew there was no way out. There and then he had accepted death. With the small kids in each arm and dangling on one leg, he swayed from side to side. This went on for a long time. Udenka's siblings were watching the drama from the other end of the improvised bridge and expected the worst to happen. At last, Fidelis miraculously recovered his balance and did not topple over to drown with his two young children. He knew so much was at stake with two of his children in each hand. No human being would have come out alive falling into such a deep, rushing stream – a tragedy that would have been thought unnecessary following a trip to see the tiger killer.

Following the trip, Fidelis realised that Christmas was fast approaching and he had no money to celebrate it. He was only paid five shillings a month as head teacher. There was no money available to pay for food and a goat. It was routine in the household that a goat was slaughtered on that special day. Goats in previous years were bought in advance to announce the approaching festival. Its absence in the compound a week before Christmas brought closer to home the seriousness of the situation. There was so much anxiety affecting the entire household in an inexplicable way. Fidelis was filled with apprehension. He resorted to prayer. In the evenings he was busy praying. His long rosary would hang over his neck stretching to touch the ground, and he walked slowly, alone, around the large compound the size of a football field praying for hours on end. Three days before Christmas, the tension reached feverish pitch. The children were fidgeting and their parents were worried stiff and absorbed in thought. It was a testing time, and then something happened. There was a strange knock at the door at five o'clock in the morning, which was highly unusual in such a sleepy village. Fidelis' first reaction was not to respond to the knocking for safety reasons, but on second thought, he got up and advanced towards the door. He struggled to open the door in the dark but eventually managed to do it. To his surprise and amazement, there was a tall stranger standing in front of the door with a huge goat in his hand. When the stranger left without the goat, Fidelis woke up the entire household and urged them to come outside. When everyone saw the goat, the atmosphere in the entire household lit up. They all lined up outside in single file and, with everyone holding on to a long dry stick perched delicately on top of their heads, they danced around the compound in merriment. It was the best Christmas ever.

Chapter Five

Eventually, it was decided that Udenka was to leave home to go and live with his elder brother in a township. He was very young when he left his parents and siblings behind. He felt excited leaving home, away from the prying eyes of his strict parents, but at the same time he was sad that he was leaving behind his younger siblings. The brother he went to live with, Godwin, was a young, handsome and intelligent man. He worked full time in the government ministry as a clerk and was just starting out in life. He socialised well and was good at dancing, particularly ballroom dancing. In fact, he was out in the evenings teaching ballroom dancing in a government-sponsored social club and would come home late at night. Udenka settled down easily and learnt how to do shopping and to prepare and present cooked meals on time to his brother. He had been there for one week when one night, he went to bed, having bolted the door that led to their room, before quickly dozing off. Godwin had gone to the social club. Udenka woke up to pounding on the door in the middle of the night. He was awake enough to open the door to let Godwin in.

They lived in a single room. He left the room as his brother entered. The Gents was outside the room, so to ease oneself, one had to leave the room. Godwin, who was just let in, saw Udenka leave and assumed that he went to the Gents, but after ten minutes when he did not return, Godwin quickly realised all was not well. He rushed to the

Gents, and when Udenka was not to be found there, Godwin rushed onto the busy night street.

After Godwin had walked a short distance, he spotted Udenka walking unconcerned in the middle of the tarred road at quite a distance from him. Godwin ran fast, shouting Udenka's name out at the same time.

Udenka suddenly heard his name called only to realise he was walking in the middle of the tarred road. Godwin caught up with him and brought him back to the house. Udenka did not realise as one would expect that he had been sleepwalking. Luckily, no vehicle came along while he was sleepwalking, probably because it was late at night and there were few vehicles around.

Udenka made friends easily in his newly arrived town but discovered that to survive, he had to stand his ground. There was a lot of fighting going on among the boys in the street where he lived. As he was about to fully settle down in the township, he got involved in a fight that ended in injuries sustained by his opponent. The boy's parents marched down to where Udenka lived to complain to his brother, Godwin. That was how his brother knew about the fight. Godwin warned him seriously never to fight again. That would eventually turn out to be his last duel. He was to be accosted on several occasions that would have led to a fight, but he kept his cool.

Apart from the fight, the first six months passed smoothly. Without asking, his mates informed him of a girl just arrived from a different town. From what he could gather, everyone who spoke about her agreed she was beautiful. That was the only good thing about her, her unquestionable beauty. Otherwise, according to his mates who briefly saw her, she was rude, rough, and ready to stand her ground against boys or girls. Her name was Juliet. The meeting point for the boys and girls living in the street where Udenka resided was a tap at the end of the street, where all of them fetched water, and this was the spot where most fights took place as they often disputed whose turn it was to fetch water. Empty buckets were lined up depending on who came first and whose turn it was. It was also a spot for socialising and meeting girls, despite their innocent young age. It was there that Udenka met Juliet for the first time. He was taken aback by her attractiveness and her watchful eyes. He marvelled at her well-sculpted face and could not stop looking at her from a safe distance. Her movements were smooth and elegant. She was ever so proud and conscious of her beauty. It was felt that her aggression and rudeness was a way of keeping boys at bay. She kept her distance from the boys. Both eventually met at the pump when she asked Udenka to help her lift the bucket full of water on to her well-rounded head. From that point, they began to form a relationship that revolved around good timing and meeting each other at the pump. They got on so well with each other to the surprise of other boys and girls. Juliet knew quite a bit and was in control of things. Udenka just followed sheepishly. At the smallest opportunity in the corner of houses and when darkness had descended on chance meeting with him, she called the shots touching and stroking him. As if that was not enough, she hatched a plan that would have ended in deepening their relationship. The plan was that both were to arrive at the pump in the dark at seven o'clock in the evening, leave their bucket in the queue and move to the nearby empty school building for whatever they planned to carry out. It was a very well thought out plan. She also wanted Udenka to arrive first, drop his bucket and quietly move to the school without been seen. She would do the same ten minutes later and join him there. It looked like a flawless arrangement.

On the appointed day and time, Udenka arrived first and found the pump busy and full of young boys his age. He was very young at the time. He dropped his bucket and made a clandestine circuitous movement to the lonely school compound and entered the school building. The wall of the school building did not reach the ceiling but left a wide gap. He stood silently inside the building and waited, breathing heavily in anticipation. It took another ten minutes of waiting before Juliet who was same very young age as Udenka entered the building in a rush. It was dead quiet. No sound could be heard, so it seemed. They hugged each other excitedly and were lowering themselves gently on the floor with her skirt hoicked when both out of nowhere suddenly heard shouting and running footsteps approaching the building. They both hurriedly got up. At that moment, the footsteps of screaming boys reached the entrance of the building, Udenka leapt like a lion through the gap on the wall in the dark and landed on messy sewage piled on the ground, got up and raced away. He was so fast in jumping over that high wall. No way could he have done it under any other circumstances. He could not remember how he got cleaned up.

Still a child, he was so selfish and never gave a thought about what could have happened to that beautiful Juliet. He thought there could have been over ten boys from the screaming and noise they made. He did not try to find out what actually happened to her. They did not see each other again after that; Juliet virtually disappeared. He never once heard any story relating to the incident to help him find out what happened to her. Juliet must have been moved to another town if she wasn't raped or killed that night by the marauding gang. Months later, he narrated the story to his close friends and they vehemently blamed him for not

standing up to save the girl. How could he? There were so many boys. They must have seen her leaving the water pump and quietly followed her without her realising she was been followed. It took him months to recover from the incident.

He loved his life in the township and was happy living with his brother, Godwin. Things moved at a faster pace compared to village life he was used to prior to coming to the township. He had become a good cook and visitors enjoyed his cooking.

Chapter Six

One evening, Udenka had just finished cooking food and was loitering around the house when he was taken aback by the sudden arrival of his father, Fidelis, with a group of men. One of the men was his father's closest friend, Luke, who was quite rich and had a fleet of lorries that he used as commercial vehicles. One of his vehicles was used for the trip. Luke was to play another important role later on. They had covered seventy miles. The suddenness of the visit was strange and baffling. On second look at the group, Udenka had no doubt in his mind that something was amiss. Fidelis rarely travelled out of his station. How come Fidelis had this group with him? Udenka and his brother Godwin did not know in advance they were coming. It was totally unexpected. The group looked rather strange and tense. They were saying little as if in shock. They were rather saying nothing and all had strange fixated looks. Fidelis in particular was in a bad state of mind. His eyes were red and swollen. It looked as if he had been crying for a time. Udenka could see tears in his eyes. His dad looked very withdrawn. He had never seen his courageous father cry before or look the way he appeared now.

It took the group time to summon up courage to ask Udenka the whereabouts of his brother, Godwin. Before the people in the group could say a thing, they made sure they sat Fidelis down, sandwiched between two men who held him tightly. Udenka told them Godwin had gone to the government recreation club where he taught ballroom dancing. They looked incredulous and seemed not to take this in, as if it was not the news they had anticipated. They had these frozen faces that seemed not to show any expression. When given the news that Godwin was fine, Fidelis' mood did not lift and he remained distraught. He then opened his mouth for the first time and said that until his son, Godwin, was physically brought in front of him, he wouldn't believe anything. Udenka was given the task of going to fetch his brother. As the group waited anxiously, they became increasingly tense, and withheld any form of conversation; so much was at stake. When Udenka finally entered the room with his brother, Godwin, the entire group came alive. Fidelis felt happy and relieved. He relaxed and began to talk excitedly. The group then began to narrate what the fuss was all about. A telegram sent to Fidelis had been the source of the commotion and grief. Telegrams were the main source of fast communication at that period. It was a sad story. Udenka's very intelligent cousin had gone to the UK on student scholarship. He had left his only twelve-year-old son behind. Within six months of arriving in the UK, his son, Sony, suddenly took ill and died soon after. A telegram was sent from the village post office to Fidelis by his brother to inform him about the sudden death. Unfortunately, the telegram read "SON DIED" instead of Sony died. Udenka's dad, Fidelis, rightly assumed that his son, with whom he had spent so much time, bringing up and educating, had passed away. He went through hell caused by the omission of one letter. The group told the two siblings that they were unable to control Fidelis all through the journey. Now relieved, they quickly got up and departed for the long journey back.

Udenka was not doing well in his new school. He had other distractions and rarely studied or did his homework. He was carried away by activities in the township compared to quiet village life. He hardly stayed at home. He preferred loitering around street corners with his male friends and classmates. The one he spent the most time with had rich parents and was very spoilt. One day, he asked Udenka to escort him to a certain place. He gave little details and did not mention the exact place they were going or what the visit was for. Udenka just followed him. After all, they were classmates. They walked casually along well-known streets saying little to each other. When they covered about two miles, his friend made a quick turn and before Udenka could realise it, they were inside a large rectangular room with single chairs arranged tightly in all the four corners. Apart from the chairs, there was no other furniture to fill the wide space. All the seats were occupied by boys of various ages who were now gazing at the new entrants. Udenka could recognise only one person and had learnt from his colleagues that he was a drug addict. The fact that this character was in the mist of this group sent shivers down his spine. The front door was then closed, and without a sound from any of those gathered together, the addict began to pass round wrapped-up stuff, emitting smoke from one end that did not look like a cigarette. Udenka would easily recognise a cigarette if he saw one because a smoker lived in his yard. The stuff began to be passed from one person to the other. Each person who handled it smoked and inhaled before passing it to the next person. It moved slowly clockwise, starting from the row opposite Udenka. The place was dead quiet; no voice could be heard from the gathering. Halfway through the group, it was Udenka's turn to handle the stuff and all eyes were on him. He was so small and young but there and then, even though he was taken by surprise, he had worked out what to do. He was very tough inside, but externally, it appeared as if he was weak. He adamantly refused to handle it. All attention was now directed towards him and he saw the wicked look in their eyes, but he was unbowed. At this point, everyone started to shout at him and abuse him. The next thing he knew, they were physically upon him. He was manhandled and quickly thrown out onto the street, beaten up and bruised. Udenka never again spoke to the friend who took him there. When he got home, he never told his older brother about the incident that had shaken him.

There was something else that occupied Udenka's time. He spent time and time with Ifeoma who was much older than him.

Ifeoma lived twenty houses away from Udenka on the same street. He couldn't remember exactly how he came to know her. It was in the late forties. She was a tall, well-crafted teenage girl, stunning in a multi-coloured, long gown. People living around her were fond of her, attracted by her elegance, smooth, cheerful face and stunning beauty. Her long, well-shaped legs were a source of great admiration. She walked with graceful long strides with a tilt of her left hip as if about to break into a dance. Her gait gave a false impression of one looking for a date. Ifeoma became so fond of Udenka that she went everywhere with him. Every Sunday at lunchtime with him in tow, hand in hand, they took off on an adventure that would last several hours. They covered quite a distance on foot to get to other part of the township where mostly young traders lived alone, usually in flats. They moved from one street to the other. She was so smart and knew a lot of the traders. They were hopping from one flat to another. Upon entering the flat of each young male,

Udenka was immediately sat down in the lounge, abandoned with a bowl full of biscuits. She would emerge eventually and they were soon out on the street, only to walk into another house. She knew them all. It came to an end after visiting over ten houses each occupied by an unmarried, single male. They visited them one at a time in different locations, close to one another. Exhausted, both walked back slowly to their own part of town, saying little to one another on their way home. It was the same every Sunday and he looked forward to more biscuits; he couldn't give a damn what went on during those visits as long as he filled his stomach with biscuits. On a few occasions, he was sick on the way back having consumed so much. This lifestyle with the teenage girl was short-lived because as one would expect, she developed early morning sickness. Her parents disowned her and she escaped to the village to sit out the embarrassment she caused her parents. His source of biscuits came to an end and Ifeoma saw him no more.

Chapter Seven

It did not surprise Udenka that he failed the promotional examination to the next class. He was the only one who had failed the examination in his entire class. The following year, the rest moved to the next class while he was to repeat. Even though he failed his examination, he told himself that he was not the one to be left behind. When he got to school on the first day of the new term, he waited for one hour and then moved unexpectedly to the new class of his classmates who were promoted. They all knew he had failed the promotional examination and should not be there and even though they were all aggravated by his presence, they were merely eyeing the small and likeable figure angrily. He was settling down at the front desk despite grumbling from his peers. They were still considering throwing him out but were soon overtaken by events. Udenka was in the new class barely thirty minutes when they saw two large school inspectors approaching aggressively and quickly the front of the class where Udenka was sitting from the opposite direction. They were coming routinely to check on anyone who shouldn't be in the class. Pupils at the back of the class shouted, "Hide him! Hide him." He was so small that his classmates managed to hide him in the front row, as it was easier to do so because they were taken by surprise. Udenka was surprised about how his peers responded quickly to save him rather than point him out to the inspectors. Not a single person betrayed him in the whole class. He remained in the new class until the next promotional examination at the end of the year.

Attendance at school was regular until one day a pupil from the senior class threatened him at the gate, saying he was going to wait for him at the school exit to beat him up at the end of the day's lectures. He was so scared by this real threat that he left school early that day, allowing enough time for school closure. He took the threat so seriously that for several months he was not seen in the classroom. He left home every day dressed for school, only to drop his schoolbag at the gate and wander through town plucking mangoes from trees and whiling away his time in other ways. He would pick up his bag from the school gate nearing the end of school time and head for home. Godwin never knew Udenka wasn't attending lectures. He would come home in school uniform pretending to Godwin as if he was genuinely attending classes. Not surprisingly, he was eventually expelled from school just before his final year. That didn't bother him, for he was already thinking of an apprenticeship in tailoring. There was a famous tailor, Eugene, living in the same compound as Udenka who had trained well abroad. Eugene was well known and made designer suits. Udenka was close to him and adored him. He had indicated to this well-trained tailor and friend his intention to train under him and eventually become a tailor, but he received a lukewarm response, which surprised Udenka. The cool response was not enough to dissuade him. He had a very strong relationship with Eugene and undertook regular errands for him and his girlfriend, Peggy. She was so fond of Udenka that there was nothing she wouldn't do for him. He became intimate with the couple and took an interest in them, so he knew what was going on in the pair's relationship.

One evening, the couple started to get ready for a party in the city hall that would involve a lot of ballroom dancing. The tailor, Eugene, was turned out in an immaculate blue suit that fit his small rounded body. His red, smooth shirt and black silk tie dazzled. Peggy was a young lady of flawless beauty dressed in a flowing ballroom gown that fit her carefully proportioned, slim body. Her platform shoes exaggerated her height and gave her extra elegance.

Udenka saw them off. They were holding hands and smiling as they went out of sight. Udenka was in full admiration and wished he was old enough to attend such a ball with his girlfriend, like the couple he had just seen off.

He went to bed as soon as the couple left for the party as it was nearing ten o'clock at night. He woke up around midnight to ease himself and on walking back, he suddenly saw Eugene, the tailor, approaching the long corridor to his room, looking downtrodden and without Peggy. He inquired about her only to be told what had happened at the ballroom dance party. According to Eugene, she started dancing continuously with one man, ignoring him, and eventually followed this new man home. Udenka found it difficult to comprehend the story. He began to wonder how a girl could treat a man so badly as to abandon him on the dance floor. Both partners had lived together for six months and adored each other. She stayed with the man she had met on the dance floor for three months. When she finally returned to the yard, Eugene started beating and flogging her so mercilessly over a prolonged period that Udenka ran into the room, as small as he was, crying loudly and shouting repeatedly, "You will kill her, you will kill her," "You will kill her." There was no one in the entire yard but Udenka at the time. He could do nothing to stop it. Udenka cried so much because he loved her and she loved him. When the beating eventually ended, she was bundled off to where she had come from.

Udenka found it hard to understand how a man could take his loved one to a party and just lose her like that. Eugene eventually found a nice girl with whom he lived happily ever after.

Udenka was not the first child his parents had sent to live with someone else. His immediate older brother, James, had left home a year earlier to live with his paternal grandmother. It was a very testing time for him. He was a bit naïve and allowed his grandmother to control his life completely. She was a mischievous old lady who lived alone and made a lot of money selling dry fish. She was quite rich by village standards and wore gold trinkets on her ankles. The gold trinkets jingled as she walked slowly in a stooped posture. She treated James so badly that she made sure he was unable to attend school. She would send him to a faraway stream with a basket full of clothing for washing. He would spend a whole day washing up in the stream until late, by which time school was over. The next day, a new task would be manufactured in order to again stop him from attending school. She devised all sorts of maltreatments. She would not provide him with regular meals and he was virtually starving. Being young and inexperienced, he was incapable of devising evasive action to try and save himself. During the period in question, news travelled slowly as postal services were not efficient and there was no telephone system. People travelled less as there were few vehicles. His father did not bother to find out what was happening to the son he sent to live with his mother. The boy was slowly wasting away. Parents felt it was part of a child's learning process, the harsher the treatment, the better for the child's maturity.

Parents usually turned a blind eye. His nearest sibling was Godwin who was then a student at the time in question in a college in another town not far away. A message finally got to him, as he was the nearest, that James was about to die if not quickly removed from his grandmother. He travelled to his hometown and picked up his sibling and they both travelled back to the city with the little money he had. James was emaciated, withdrawn and said little. When they got to town, they moved to the motor park to join a lorry going to their parent's station about sixty miles away. While waiting for the lorry to be fully loaded with passengers, they sat on the floor with other passengers and were served a pre-paid cooked meal. They all ate in the small space allocated and the place was crowded. As they ate, closely packed on the floor in the open space, James inadvertently dipped his food into the bowl of a man eating alone next to the two brothers. James' older brother, Godwin, apologised to the man unreservedly, hoping that would end the matter, but the man was relentless. He blew the minor incident out of proportion and insisted the contaminated soup be replaced. People around begged and begged the man so much but he refused. James and his brother had little money. It was rather unfortunate. Eventually, people began to contribute just enough money to replace the soup.

James was warmly received by his siblings and parents. He was emaciated and said little about his treatment. He was enrolled in school and was happy that he no longer lived with his grandmother. He was withdrawn, scared, and psychologically and emotionally damaged. He was intelligent but not smart enough. This incident happened a month after he was removed from his grandmother. There was a popular stream not far from where they lived, often visited by the villagers to bathe and swim. There were two sections of the stream separated by a giant tree trunk placed across it. It demarcated one section that was shallow, meant for those who could not swim, and a deep section for people who could swim well. Villagers who wanted to get into the deep end stood on the trunk and then dived in. The trunk was easily crowded with people trying to plunge in. On this particular day, the trunk was overcrowded. Godwin, who brought James back from their hometown, was a good swimmer and was beginning to feel impatient over the overcrowding for he had no space to stand. Suddenly, he noticed that James, with no swimming experience whatsoever, was standing on the tree trunk for no understandable reason. He shouted at him to dive in and when he did not, he pushed him into the deep section. Udenka was close by and watched the drama unfold. He knew James could not swim and would soon drown. Godwin, who pushed James into the deep section, cautiously stood on the trunk and waited for James to surface, but when he did not, he dived in. People waited for four anxious minutes, when suddenly, they saw James being pushed under water from behind by Godwin to the shallow side of the stream. When he was brought out, he was unconscious with water coming out of his mouth. Villagers surrounded him and tried to resuscitate him. He eventually regained consciousness and was extremely lucky not to have drowned. His brother, Godwin, who pushed him into the deep end, warned all the siblings present not to say a thing to their parents. It became a well-kept secret but not for very long. Udenka, overburdened by the secret he was carrying, spilled it and his parents came to know but were unable to imagine the gravity of the situation at the time.

Chapter Eight

Udenka remained at home still living with Godwin for nearly nine months, refusing to attend school and hoping to be trained as a tailor when, suddenly, his father, Fidelis recalled him. He had to return to where he had started life to resume his schooling. While he was away, the family had moved to another town, but the school headed by his dad did not have primary six for those in the final year of first school. He had to be registered at the school that his dad headed for five years before he was transferred to the new school eight miles away. He had to go from home each morning, riding a bike along a sandy road with high hills and dangerously sharp corners. The road was so lonely and only dominated by his presence and the sharp descents and ascents of hills.

Towards evening, his parents would begin to worry and look out for his safe return.

This village where he attended school had a problem with mad dogs. The entire village was in constant mourning with people dying of rabies. He could often hear people who developed rabies barking like mad dogs. Once he was chased by a rabid dog for miles while cycling home from school. The dog wouldn't give up but carried on in its pursuit. He had to climb up the bike to stand on the seat while in motion and then stretch to reach a low tree branch that was hanging down low enough to be within reach. When he was satisfied he had a firm hold on the branch, he released the bicycle. He eventually climbed onto the tree trunk and up to a safe height. The dog patiently waited for him to climb down. An elderly man passing by noticed his predicament and chased the dog away.

This village and surrounding town seemed to have had this problem with rabid dogs for a few years now. Udenka recalled, a few years back, when they were living in the village, what happened to the dog his parents owned. It was a friendly pet and he was so fond of it, often taking it for a walk. It rarely ventured out alone. His father came home one day to announce that a few of their neighbours' dogs had become infected. Within days of learning about the problem, their own dog, which normally stayed at home, wandered off and did not return for days. It was very unusual for this dog. His dad noticed quickly that the dog was behaving strangely when it got back. His parents gathered Udenka and his siblings into a room, locking them in for safety. The parents then managed to finally round up their favourite pet and killed it, as it had become infected while mixing with other rabid dogs for the three days it was out of the house.

Udenka was well settled in his new school and was happy with the long bicycle ride. First term in the school went smoothly and he soon found himself on midterm holidays.

Two days later, he was sent into the village on an errand by his father. His father liked sending him because he was good at riding a bicycle and clever in delivering any message efficiently. His father would send no one else but him. He rode off that sunny afternoon at speed, cruising through the narrow footpath uninterrupted. As he rode along, he met no one on the footpath and then remembered it was a big market day and everybody had departed early to be at the market. He was singing and talking to himself when out of nowhere he saw a long, black, deadly snake stretched across the footpath, motionless under a tree shadow, avoiding the harsh sunshine and cooling off. It was too late to take evasive action. He could not avoid it. He rode straight over it in the middle of the motionless snake and thought it was the end. He quickly looked back to see if it was dead. To his utter surprise, the snake had come alive and was chasing him. He pedalled fast, but the snake was on his heels. It chased and chased him for quite a distance before giving up and retiring into the bush. He felt relieved but exhausted. On his way back, with trepidation he passed the very spot where he had seen the snake. When he got home, he was too frightened to tell his parents or siblings what he had experienced and kept it to himself.

Udenka continued to ride back and forth to the faraway school without any incidents on the way until the end of the year.

Chapter Nine

When all seemed fine, Fidelis suddenly took ill with high fever that stretched for over a week. On the second week, his condition worsened and he felt worse. At that point, Fidelis realised that he was so ill he was unlikely to recover. Twice, he took Udenka to a nearby classroom and stood by the side of the blackboard with a white chalk in one hand to write or tell him important family-related things short of writing a will, but couldn't. Udenka knew his dad wanted to tell him things but felt he was too young. His dad did not realise how mature his son was. He felt sorry for his dad not knowing how living in the township had matured his young son. How could he tell his sick dad he was ready for anything? Fidelis was not aware his son had inner strength and could take anything on board. Unfortunately, Fidelis could not tell this little boy a thing. He was too ill and lacked the courage to tell him and this pained Udenka. He did not know how to urge him on to tell him. He nearly did the second time around. The boy was so ready for it.

Just before his father took ill, Udenka started to spend the night in another young teacher's house, about a hundred yards away. His parents allowed this to ease overcrowding. He slept on the same bed with the teacher. One night, during the second week of his father's illness, he was startled and woken up by the teacher, screaming in the early hours of the morning. The teacher woke him up and told the little boy that he dreamt that Fidelis had died. The teacher started crying. Udenka was as cool as ever and said nothing. Both rushed to Udenka's house to find that his dad's illness had worsened and he had become delirious, Udego by his side. The teacher Udenka slept with was asked by Udego to ride to a small township six miles away to call Fidelis's closest friend, Luke. Luke arrived in his vehicle and took Udenka's parents to his house in the small township. Udenka and the teacher rode to the town later on a bicycle. Luke went with Udenka to see a doctor working in a nearby hospital and both asked him to pay a home visit. The doctor arrived within three hours and, after examining Fidelis still delirious, said nothing could be done to save him and left to go back to the hospital. Fidelis passed away soon after.

Udenka and the teacher were outside inside a pickup truck belonging to Luke pondering what would inevitably happen next. Someone came out to give them the bad news, and the teacher burst out crying and remembered what he saw in his dream the night before. Udenka showed no emotion. It was too much for him. Both quickly moved into the house to witness what had happened. The dead father, Fidelis, was on the bed surrounded by a weeping wife and crying family friends. It was not a good sight. It was a really bad day, heavy rain falling continuously and pelting the zinc roof. The teacher next to Udenka continued crying, but Udenka remained cool and collected even though sad. The teacher looked at him for a second time and couldn't believe he was the only one not crying. His eyes were as dry as ever. He was preoccupied with something that needed urgent attention. He was thinking not about the sudden loss but how to arrange for his dad to be taken home to his hometown and people, hundred miles away, to be formally buried. That was all he was thinking about. His dad needed to be taken to his homeland for burial. He needed to be with his own people. Udenka was very young at the time. Luke was next to his dead friend, holding his hand, crying at the same time. It was a very moving site. Udenka's eldest sibling Godwin, who lived eighty miles away, arrived four hours later and Udenka went outside to meet him, and, when he told him that their dad was no more alive, he broke down naturally.

Being the eldest, Godwin understood the dire situation. His dad, Fidelis, was now dead leaving behind a young housewife and ten young children. He realised the responsibility thrust upon him at a very young age, an ordinary clerk in the ministry. The family was badly hit. Four weeks previously, they were gathering things and getting excited about the plan to visit home for Christmas when suddenly the breadwinner became ill. With everyone around Udenka weeping, he remained collected and focused. He walked up to his dad's friend, Luke, the transporter, who was beside his dead father crying and told him he wanted him to arrange the transportation of his dead father to his hometown to be amongst his own people and relatives prior to burial. Luke looked at Udenka and could not believe what he was seeing and hearing from the little boy. Luke did exactly what Udenka told him. He organised two vehicles to take family belongings and the body to Udenka's native land where the burial took place. There, Luke was telling Udenka's people that the little boy was the one who organised to bring his father home.

There followed a period of immense suffering and wretchedness for Udenka and his entire family. He had just finished first school. There was no money for him to go to a secondary school, and, as such, he did not apply for a place. It was becoming obvious that he would remain at home in his hometown for at least a year doing nothing. Then the unexpected happened. A young girl, Lucy, from a nearby town arrived at the house to meet the bereaved. Lucy happened to know Godwin, Undenka's brother. She had one gap year before going to university. She was very young, beautiful, pleasant, soft spoken and very fluent in English. She was smart, intelligent and unbelievably kind hearted. This was her first visit to the house. She was so moved by what she saw that she decided to take one child, and that child was Udenka. Lucy had recently been accepted to teach at a mixed college in a quite distant place. How could a young girl just out of secondary school take such a big responsibility of looking after a small boy not remotely related to her? That was what she did.

A day was fixed when Udenka would be picked up by Lucy for the onward journey to the college. It was a long and difficult trip. He arrived with Lucy late at night to be welcomed warmly by the principal of the college and the rest of his staff. Udenka felt very privileged to be received like that. He started schooling in earnest the next day but lived with Lucy in staff accommodation for a term before moving to the dormitory. In the dormitory, things were different. Life appeared more regimented and things were done in an orderly fashion; for example, there was a fixed time to go to bed and no talking after that. There was a classmate whose bed was close to his. This boy would wake up in the middle of the night screaming so loudly as to wake everyone in the dormitory. He regularly had nightmares and it was quite terrifying the way he would scream. Udenka would wake up in a jolt of fear. Sleep was interrupted on a nightly basis. The boy would become so agitated following the screaming that people near him would jump out of bed to hold him in case he injured himself, and console him and calm him down. This very boy went home at the end of term, and when he came back to school the following term, he brought four full packets of sugar in cube form. He started consuming lots of sugar. Udenka kept warning him about the health risks, but he remained adamant and kept eating excess sugar. He developed diabetes mellitus after two terms in school and never came back. The school learnt that he had passed away at home. Unfortunately, he was no longer there to wake them up during his horrible nightmares. Udenka remained in the school for nine months and when Lucy moved to study at the university, Udenka moved to a new school nearer home. Lucy looked after him so well and supported him financially and in many other ways that he missed her. Her timely appearance like a Good Samaritan soon after the death of Fidelis was a saviour. Udenka was most vulnerable at the time following the sudden bereavement that, without Lucy, he no doubt would have gone off the rails. She was eventually to marry a famous Nigerian writer.

Chapter Ten

During the school holidays, Udenka would live with Udego in the village. He was now maturing and capable of helping her more in the farm and going on errands for her also, particularly taking messages to his grandmother. He remembered an incident that happened one day he was taking food to his grandmother two and half miles away. It was late morning. He set off alone and walked along the narrow footpath lined with prickly leaves and thorns. One mile into the journey on this quiet, peaceful village route, he saw two girls standing alone in front of a house talking and whispering to each other intensely as if they were hatching a plot. One had come to visit the other and they appeared to be of similar age as Udenka, fast approaching adolescent period. He could recognise one of them from a distance. Both girls were standing in front of the house of the girl he was able to recognise from a distance. They beckoned to him to come closer and he did so. They asked him to walk with them into a bush but did not give a reason for venturing into a thick uninhabited forest. The two girls walked briskly in front, as if in a hurry, and he followed behind. The girls were the same height, light-skinned, smart and noticeably well shaped. The one Udenka recognised was rough, and he had seen her often in fights in the village with girls her age. In one of the fights he witnessed, she stripped the girl she fought with stark naked in public in a flash like a lightning strike, and it took the poor innocent girl time to realise she was now unclothed. It was awful. The girl now completely conquered, shamed and humiliated ran away for shelter. Udenka was afraid of the wild girl and felt intimidated in her presence. They trudged along silently. Suddenly, they reached a clearing in the thick bush. They spent some time there playing within the two girls term of engagement. In the end, the girls got up quickly and walked off abruptly, irritated and disappointed at dealing with a stupid novice. The two girls never spoke to him again. Whenever any of them walked past him in the village in the subsequent days and months, they behaved similarly: they swore at him and spat on the ground as he passed. He felt so humiliated; so much so that until now he felt so ashamed that he never told the story.

School holidays with his mother were never like a vacation. It meant spending so much time on the farm with her and the other siblings. He hated it and tried to find ways to escape to the township, if only he could find somewhere to stay. His elder brother, Godwin, was now at university so he was living on campus in a different town, but his friend, Clement, still lived in the township and asked Udenka to visit him. He had little money for transport to travel to the township from the village several miles away. Luckily, one weekend, his cousin, Vincent, came to the village from the township in his car and Udenka went to his house nearby to ask for a lift. He was a nice cousin and very approachable. He agreed to give Udenka a lift the next day but warned him that his car had no brakes except for the handbrake. For Udenka, what was most important to him was to escape home and farm work. The fact that the vehicle had no brakes did not concern him or ring any warning bell. He was just too young to process the implications. He knew nothing about cars. As young as he was, he never thought of death. The next day, they took off and he sat excitedly in the front seat and needed no reminding about the situation with the vehicle. In less than two miles, the precarious situation he was in was brought nearer home when the vehicle was unable to stop behind a stationary lorry to allow the vehicle coming from the opposite direction to pass. Instead, Vincent drove into the path of the oncoming trailer, which swerved into the bush to avoid them. The handbrake could not stop the vehicle. It was at that point that Udenka realised they were staring death in the eye and he was no longer comfortable. Along the way, there were several misses and his heart was in his mouth. As they were approaching a familiar junction nine miles into town, they knew they were coming to the most dangerous part of the road – a part that was dreaded by every motorist, notorious for several accidents and deaths. All along the journey, Udenka was thinking only about that stretch of road. He was convinced they would end up there, dead. The remaining nine miles were renowned for a steep descent, numerous hairpin bends and a deep, bottomless valley on the left-hand side of the road that had swallowed several fallen vehicles in the past. When they got there, as luck would have it, there was a big accident and the road was blocked, resulting in a tailback of over fifty vehicles. On arrival at the spot, their vehicle, as expected, was unable to stop. It started hitting stationary vehicles until it came to a stop. Luckily, they did not end up in the gorge, but his cousin Vincent was nearly lynched by vehicle owners whose vehicles were damaged by him. Vincent's break-less car managed to hit and damage ten stationary vehicles before it could come to a halt. When the road eventually opened, Udenka hitched a ride into town in another vehicle and eventually ended up in Clement's apartment.

Clement was a character. He was tall, well-shaped, very handsome and spoke in a low voice. He communicated well and was fashionable. Girls loved him and ran after him. He lived in a single room and had no means of existence. He, however, managed to survive somehow supported by his numerous girlfriends. At times he took money from their handbags when they were not looking. An act he so perfected. Udenka saw it happen a number of times and each time he stood there dumbfounded. It did not surprise him when Clement took the little money Udenka had with him and they survived on it. The money he had was given to him by Udego for transport to use on the return journey. The money soon ran out and there was nothing left for feeding or to use to return to the village. He was trapped there for several days. Every day he was promised money by Clement, but the promise was not kept. In the end, Udenka moved into Vincent's single-room accommodation in another part of town as he couldn't find money to return to the village. One morning, when Vincent had gone to work, Clement suddenly walked into the room. He handed Udenka his bicycle key and ordered him to go to the front of the house to bring in the bicycle parked and locked outside. The corridor was long and Vincent's room was situated at the rear end. Udenka was smart and thought very fast. He knew that Clement should not be left alone for long in the room. He dashed outside and to save time, rather than struggle to open the bike lock with the keys, he hurriedly lifted the back of the bicycle and rolled it through the corridor in a jiffy. When he got back to the room, Clement was taken aback because he was caught digging his hands in the inside pocket of Vincent's-suit in the wardrobe. There was no purpose to his visit but to pilfer. When Vincent returned from work, Udenka told him what had happened and advised him to check his suit pockets in case something was missing.

The new school was a Roman Catholic college and, as such, much stricter than his previous mixed college. The principal was a tall Irish priest supported by four other priests of the same nationality. Morning mass was compulsory and group prayers were said several times during the day. The dress code was strict. He struggled financially and often had nothing. He was very much supported by his new friend, Cyril, whose father was a businessman with plenty of money. They lived close to one another in the dormitory and did things together all through the college years and never said anything bad about each other. On one occasion, the school vacated for summer holidays and Udenka had no money to go back to the village several miles away to be with his mother and siblings. Cyril came to his aid and paid for his transport home. That was not the first time Cyril bailed him out. It happened so often. He found himself at the back of an articulated lorry jam packed with passengers, including children, men and women.

He was sitting close to the entrance of the vehicle, sandwiched between two adults. The man who sat on his right was huge and wore long white robes. Udenka thought he was from the northern part of the country. The man sat still as they travelled along, looking straight at the twisting road and causing no problem to anyone. In contrast, the man who sat on Udenka's left came from a different part of the country, noted for outspokenness, and as such he never stopped talking. Not only was he talking, he was constantly pouring abuse on the gentleman in the white robe, who kept quiet, supposedly unconcerned. When the other passengers could no longer take the talking and abuse directed at one person from another tribe, they started to warn the talkative but he paid no heed. Then suddenly, in a flash, the serene gentleman in the white robe flashed a long, shiny, well-polished sword in the air. The speed at which he pulled it out was amazing. When Udenka saw the massive, sharp, threatening sword next to him, he froze with fear. He thought he was going to be beheaded there and then. He nearly wet his pants but then remembered he was not wearing any. The other passengers weighed down on the man with the drawn sword begging him to put it down. It was so scary. No one knew or had anticipated that he had such a big knife with him. The loud man with the foul mouth kept quiet for the rest of the journey.

Following the long vacation, which Udenka quite enjoyed, he got back to college and resumed work in earnest.

There was a girls' college nearby that had a good relationship with the boys' school Udenka was attending. It was always exciting whenever the two schools met. It happened infrequently and during the Holy Week of Easter when both schools went to the town church for services. His childhood sweetheart was at that girls' school. Her name was Nancy. They lived in the same township. Nancy's father was the boss of Udenka's brother, Godwin. Her father used to send her on errands to Godwin with messages relating to departmental work. When they were small children, they liked each other and related well. Nancy was quite fair and was blessed with a very beautiful face. She was well-behaved and predictable. They did not see each other often as kids, only when she was sent to deliver a message. With both now in secondary school, they began to see each other more often and frequently exchanged love letters. Nancy wrote beautiful letters in well-crafted handwriting in blue ink. He read them repeatedly. Her letters were arriving on a frequent basis. He could not now remember how the letters were delivered to him. He kept all the letters in the classroom locker that had a lock. His classmates knew about the letters because during lessons and studies he would open them, bend over them and read, quietly concentrating. A boy from Nancy's town who knew about the relationship was in his class. The boy's brother was also interested in Nancy. One evening, Udenka got to his class and noticed the locker had been broken into and all her letters had disappeared. He was devastated. He had hoped the relationship would result in marriage when they got older. She never forgave him. She blamed him for leaving such letters in the classroom. They never saw each other again. He found it so difficult to deal with the loss. He began to lose concentration and interest in his studies. It took him several months to pull himself together. He was ever so young to face such a loss. He felt it was extremely wicked of her to treat him the way she did and for refusing to forgive him. She literally dropped him just like that.

One morning, during his second year at the school, he coughed and the spit contained a tiny streak of blood, but only one time. He was having nosebleeds at the time because he was mistakenly punched in the nose. Being a child, he panicked and went to his chemistry teacher, who was an Irish priest and his housemaster. He asked him to come back the next morning. The following day he went to the priest's house. He sat him down and disappeared. He was back in five minutes with a cup of cold milk that Udenka drank very quickly. It was so tasty; he wished he would be offered more.

He was then bundled into a car and they drove off, destination unknown. It was over an hour's journey with the Irish priest in the driving seat. He said nothing to his young passenger all the way to their destination. When the vehicle eventually stopped, he suddenly realised that his housemaster had driven him to a hospital with an isolation unit. The building that housed the isolation unit was isolated from the rest of the hospital and was actually in the middle of nowhere. He just dumped him there and drove off.

The isolation ward was full of adult patients seriously ill. He was the only child in the unit and was sent up and down on errands by older patients. He spent seven days in the unit and the only visitor he had throughout this period was his mum, who came once, having covered about seventy miles. The housemaster, after dumping him at the hospital, did not once return to check how he was getting on. Udenka was so well to be in a place like that but learnt so much by observing people who were genuinely ill unlike himself and saw first-hand how their illness affected them.

Patients were dying around him despite treatment. Even though he saw many deaths in the days he was there, he was so moved by the death of a man whose bed was next to him that Udenka took his on discharge and went back to his school. He did not want ever to see his schoolmaster again.

Chapter Eleven

Udenka's attitude towards his studies changed as he became older and more mature. He became more studious and developed interests in the sciences and was once asked by his elder brother, Godwin, what his future career would be. He quickly retorted that he wanted to be a rocket scientist. His brother burst out laughing. At the time, there was a great deal of interest in space exploration and he read about space rockets in his spare time. He was of average intelligence and remained in the middle in a class of thirty students. You wouldn't regard him as being clever. Despite this, he had the ambition to move on to university. This meant finding another school for an 'A' level course. He applied for admission to a government college for that purpose. Luckily, he was invited for an entrance examination and interview while still in the final year at his current school.

He arrived at the government college the day before the entrance examination. It was almost a day's journey. As he ambled aimlessly along the corridor admiring the beautiful school, he was cornered by a short boy who had come for the same entrance examination from a very good school. Udenka's school was not that good, he already knew. The boy did look handsome but had spots on his face. He asked Udenka which secondary school he came from. He told him and the boy burst out laughing uncontrollably. When he had finished laughing, he straightened up and asked Udenka what he was doing in the present location, as it was a waste of time coming because he wouldn't pass the entrance examination. He said, "If I were you, I would pack my things and go home." He was joined by a huge boy from his school who assisted him in the taunting. They went as far as discussing what games were not played in Udenka's school. In Udenka's school, football was the only game played. Numerous games were played in the two boys' school, including hockey and cricket. Udenka felt empty and washed out. He excused himself and retired to his room. He hardly slept and thought of how bad and poorly equipped his school was. He was made a laughing stock.

The next morning, the entrance examination began in earnest. They started with the first paper that would last for three hours. The hall was packed. From where he sat, Udenka could see the seating position of the two boastful boys. He found the questions hard, and he was battling with the second of five questions with only one hour gone, when the pair threw their pens up high in the air to indicate that they had done the five questions in record time and were ready to leave the examination hall. Udenka could not believe it. He was still stuck with the second question and the remaining three were equally hard. He was distracted by the two pen throwers who left the hall and lost concentration and any hope of passing the examination.

He returned to his college the next day and settled down to study for his final examination that was fast approaching. He never expected to be called for an interview as he felt he did badly in the written papers. Four weeks later, to his surprise, he was invited for the interview. Two students from his school were invited. The other invitee was his peer and was called Benjamin. He was tall and very intelligent, the son of a London-trained lawyer. Udenka knew that with Benjamin also invited for an interview, he had no chance because he was so clever and always came first in class tests and exams. Before the interview, the candidates sat on a long bench outside and were called in one by one. Benjamin went in first and was interviewed for about twenty minutes. As soon as he came out, Udenka was called in. The first question Udenka was asked was to say who was cleverer in class, himself or the lawyer's son. He knew if he answered truthfully that he had no chance whatsoever because the boy was always at the top of the class and Udenka was nowhere near him. He quickly retorted, "How could I answer that when I don't see his school report?" They burst out laughing so loudly for a long time and ended up asking him only one more question before letting him go. When he came out relieved, other candidates waiting outside to be interviewed asked him why there had been so much laughter during his interview. He knew what it was they were laughing about but could not explain it to them. The pen throwers were not seen at the interview.

Another surprise was waiting for him, for he received a letter of acceptance two weeks after his interview to do a science 'A' level course at the government college. Benjamin, who was more intelligent, was rejected only because Udenka was better at the interview and wouldn't tell the panel how clever his colleague was. He only said, "We don't share school reports. It is normally posted to parents."

Chapter Twelve

The final year at the mission, college moved rapidly and Udenka worked very hard, hoping to obtain good grades in science subjects, otherwise his place at the government college would not be retained. He did not want anything to derail his chance to start the two-year 'A' level course.

He studied unsurprisingly hard and did all to deceive his peers by giving them the impression he was not studious. During the daytime, he visibly played around and was not seen studying. At night when the rest of his peers were fast asleep, he would wake up in the early hours of the morning, lit up a lamp, covered it with a blanket over his head so that the light wouldn't be visible and he studied and studied unnoticed. The final examination came and went. He thought he had done well. School eventually vacated. He took group pictures with his peers and the next day he travelled back to the village after saying goodbye to his friend Cyril with tears in their eyes. He spent a whole month at home with Udego and his siblings before departing to start his 'A' level science course fifty miles away.

He arrived at the government college full of expectations. Being a government-run college, all facilities were in place. Several sports were available and the science departments were well equipped. The school employed well-educated teachers, some from the United Kingdom. Lectures started in earnest. He initially struggled in science, particularly physics, as his previous school had poorly-equipped laboratories.

Progress was interrupted by a large strike organised by students against the expatriate principal of the school who was eventually expelled. Lectures were suspended temporarily, and, eventually, an indigene was appointed as the principal of the school.

In the same town was a large mission hospital run by Irish Reverend Sisters. It was about a good six mile walk from the government college. It had a nursing training school within it. There were a large number of trained nurses working in the hospital as well as trainee nurses. Udenka knew a nurse from his hometown who worked in the hospital and had agreed to introduce him to one or two nurses. Portable transistor radios were very scarce at the time, but he had managed to convince his older brother Ignatius, who worked for an oil company to lend him his for a brief period. With this on hand, he set off one Sunday afternoon with a fellow schoolmate to pay a clandestine visit to the nurses. The nurses they were visiting knew beforehand about the visit. His classmate was so excited about the radio that he insisted they took it with them to show off while on the visit. It was a long walk to the hospital. On arrival at the hospital, they were directed to a reception area for the nurses. They got there and sat down and were introduced to about three nurses. The atmosphere was friendly and both visitors felt relaxed, chatting to the nurses as they were served drinks. They felt so much at home with the girls as they drank and were considering their next move, when a nurse rushed in to announce that the government college principal had suddenly arrived and was coming quickly towards reception. The two visitors grabbed their transistor radio and jumped through an open window to escape. It would have been instant expulsion had they been caught by the school authorities. Udenka wondered why the principal paid a visit, arriving there unannounced to disrupt their August visit. Both were sad as they walked home and were wondering how such a well-planned visit could end like that. They did not have a chance even to say goodbye to the girls. Both spoke little to each other as they trudged along the long stretch of lonely road back to the college.

Udenka's 'A' level course was progressing and so was his struggle with his physics 'A' level. He was comfortable with the other science subjects. He discovered that students who studied a combination of physics and mathematics found physics much easier than Udenka did. He began to spend more time in the science laboratory hoping it would make his subjects much easier. Even though he was struggling with his subjects, he found time to make friends. He befriended a student, Felix, who was two years his junior. He was tall, handsome and extremely intelligent. They became very close friends and got along well with each other. It was friendship based on trust and understanding. Felix had problem keeping to school regulations and occasionally fell fowl of the school rules and got punished. Once he returned a few days late when the school reopened. While lectures went on, he was out in the field cutting grass. The college had strict rules regarding school uniform. Students were expected to dress in a certain way to conform to the dress code, but Felix at times fell short of how he was expected to turn himself out. Shorts were supposed to be above knee length. Felix, at times to wind the principal up, wore shorts that extended far beyond the knees, and he got punished. It did not surprise Udenka to see his friend once again cutting grass in the field while the rest studied. He was one of the cleverest students Udenka ever met.

Udenka was a bit disappointed with his expected results from his last school as he was expected to score highly in the subjects he chose for the current course, but luckily he was allowed to continue. His friend, Felix, was with him when he got the results. As soon as Udenka opened the envelope and read his score, he burst into tears. It was then that he noticed that his friend, Felix, had a softer side, consoling him and showing so much empathy. He behaved like a mother would – providing tremendous support. It was a dark few days during which their friendship blossomed. Udenka reciprocated whenever his friend was punished for not sticking to college rules and was made sad by the severe punishment. He also slowly began to talk Felix out of disobeying school regulations.

Chapter Thirteen

When the school vacated for Christmas holidays, Udenka decided to spend the time with his brother, Ignatius, who worked at a drilling site for an oil company. While there one day, he decided to go and visit the children of the vice principal of his previous college. It was to be a day trip and he took off in the morning to go back home in the evening. He took the bus to his destination, a distance of forty miles. His brother escorted him to where he joined the bus and he was to be picked up at exactly the same spot upon return. The return time and pick-up location were carefully planned. Unfortunately, it all suddenly went disastrously wrong. He took a bus for the return journey but got off the bus one stop short of where he was supposed to be picked up. He did not realise he had made a mistake. There was nothing like mobile phones at the time and communication was difficult, almost impossible. He waited and waited for his brother to turn up, but he never did and it was getting darker and darker. Of course, Ignatius, was waiting at the planned location for him, not knowing that Udenka had gotten off at the wrong bus stop. When he could no longer wait for Ignatius, he decided to walk even though he did not know the terrain or in which direction to go, but he had to be on the move as it was getting dark.

The footpath was completely deserted. No soul could be seen and no sound could be heard. He walked fast. No houses could be seen. What he saw on either side was well-cultivated land of the same pattern extending for several miles on end, but there was no sign of buildings or human existence. It was getting dark very quickly and the silence was disarming. He could not think of what to do next. There was nothing else he could do really. He was in this wilderness, completely lost and with no hope of finding his way. He kept on walking for hours in the dark, aimlessly, in this uninhabited, well-cultivated, extensive land. He began to think of suicide. The loneliness in complete darkness was unbearable. The suicidal thought almost overwhelmed him. He was tiring and his legs were beginning to let him down. He started to plan how best to kill himself as he walked along. Then suddenly, out of nowhere, he began to hear distant human voices. The sound was coming from a distant direction, but he found that encouraging. Ignatius, having waited in vain where he was supposed to pick him up, had organised a search party in the village and they set off to find him. He was eventually picked up by the search party and handed over to Ignatius, who had lost all hope of finding him as the night wore thin.

Udenka eventually completed his 'A' level course and was ready to go to university. Because of the way in which university admission was planned, one would wait for approximately nine months before going to university. In the interim, Udenka applied to teach chemistry in a college and was accepted. The college was in a remotely situated small town ninety miles from his hometown. He shared a house with a fellow teacher who had arrived at the school a year earlier. He was tall, very fair and extremely fluent in the English language. He spoke rapidly but was gentle in nature, it seemed, at the time. It was a lonely life as it was quite a small town with no shops or entertainment centres. There were girls but hard to come by, as they were under the full control of their strict parents; also, being a small place, there were always the watchful eyes of the natives. There was a primary school not far from the college. He knew a few female teachers there, but they were older and more mature and did not tolerate him because of his age. They were single but treated him like the small boy he was.

His students loved his teaching and began to enjoy chemistry, which was new to the school. He worked so hard to set up a chemistry laboratory for approval by inspectors. The inspectors eventually visited and the school was granted approval for chemistry to be an official school subject. The principal, an Irish priest, was so impressed that he invited Udenka to his house for a chat. He did not know in advance what the discussion was to be about. The Irish priest started by thanking him for his hard work in setting up the chemistry department. He then touched on his main reason for the invitation. He wanted to send him to the United Kingdom to do a degree course in chemistry and to come back and teach in the college permanently. The way the principal planned to finance it was unorthodox and unusual. He would ask the villagers not to cut palm trees for three months, following which all the palm kernels would be extracted from the trees and sold to pay for Udenka's fees and all maintenance costs. Udenka listened to the suggestion but made no immediate commitment; he allowed himself to mull it over. He did not want to be permanently bound to the college, which meant living his entire life in such small town. Moreover, he wanted to study medicine and there was an impending interview for admission to medical school. When eventually he turned the request down, the principal was surprised and disappointed.

The students were so fond of attending his chemistry lectures. They worked hard and showed much interest in his subject. Udenka made chemistry look simple to draw in his students, and he succeeded in making them want to study it in the end.

There was this girl who often rode past his rented accommodation. She was so proud and never looked in his direction whenever she rode past. He came to learn that she was the older sister of one of the students he was close to. He got his friend to introduce his sister to him. Udenka came to learn she was a student in another college, miles away. Their father was a head teacher. She was not beautiful but presentable. She was cool, pleasant and communicated beautifully. She was of average height and armoured with noticeably thick lips. He invited her to his rented house when he happened to be off work. His flatmate was away at the time. She happened to be on school holidays. She arrived one morning and parked her bicycle by the side of the building. It was dead quiet and the house was isolated and stood on its own. They spent hours in the bedroom talking, cuddling, kissing and touching. They did not go beyond that because she was unwilling to go far. The mere fact that she visited was a triumph because she was such a difficult girl to corner. She eventually went home having spent nearly a whole day with him.

He was so excited and carried away by his success that he decided to tell his fellow teacher and housemate when he got back. His housemate was taken aback by his success, so much so that he found it hard to say a thing – he was speechless. He just quietly retired to his room and said nothing to Udenka. A few days later, Udenka came home and noticed the bike of his new girl parked by the side of the house. He could not comprehend what was happening. As it turned out, she was spending the same number of hours with his housemate. He could never have imagined this. He could not understand how this proud girl could humiliate him in such a raw manner. Eventually as she climbed on to her bike to ride home, Udenka looked out through the glass window to make sure he had correctly identified her. He went numb; his legs gave way and he stumbled to the ground. The next day, he confronted the housemate and there was an altercation; they were about to exchange blows when another teacher arrived and separated them. He never saw or spoke to the girl again and she was never seen in the house again. The housemates became enemies and went their separate ways. Udenka refused several attempts by others to reconcile them. They never again spoke to each other.

Chapter Fourteen

Four months after turning down the offer to study chemistry in a university in the UK, Udenka began to apply for a place at a medical school in his own country. When he was filling in the application form, he put medicine as his first choice and chemistry as his second. He was accepted without an interview to do chemistry at one of the best universities in the country but was still obsessed with a medical course. His results in the 'A' level examinations did not satisfy him, as they bordered on average and were not good enough for him to be accepted on his desired course. He repeated one of the subjects to improve his chances, and following that, he was invited to attend an interview for possible admission to a medical school two hundred miles away. He had to make the long journey. He set off early a day before the appointed date of the interview, using public transport. Along the way, he witnessed at least four fatal accidents. One of them caused the road to be closed. When he got down from the vehicle, he saw several bodies scattered by the roadside, a few still with head injuries, unconscious and twitching. People just stood there watching; there was no attempt at resuscitation at the scene and nor was there any presence of emergency services.

The road was narrow and winding. One particular stretch was the site of most accidents because, despite the road being narrow, there were several very narrow bridges appearing one after the other in a space of fifteen miles and a long, steep descent running down to end of each bridge. Accidents frequently occurred on the bridge because it could only take one vehicle at a time. Vehicles, like coaches tearing down the hill with speed from opposite sides, would kiss each other in the middle of the bridge, resulting in heavy casualties. One vehicle was supposed to stop and give way to the other. This was what happened at the spot where Udenka's journey was brought to a temporary stop. The crash was on the narrow bridge and it involved two buses laden with passengers. He was witnessing the most heart-wrenching scene. People just stood there and watched the wounded die. When the road was eventually cleared, he got back into the vehicle with a heavy heart and continued with his journey.

Udenka had his interview the following day and was accepted to commence medical training two months from the date of interview. He was very pleased with the outcome because his science results from the government college were average, but he did well at the interview and that helped to gain him a place at the school of medicine.

He made the tedious journey back to his hometown. It was the school holiday. Around the same time, his classmate living in the same village had told him that two girls who were also students had arrived at his home to spend some time with their elderly grandmother. Since they were two girl visitors, Udenka took another boy with him from the village. On their first visit, he spotted the most attractive of the two girls and navigated towards her. She had very good looks, plump, sexy and feminine. Her name was Felicia. She appeared to dominate her older sister who was short and not as attractive. Felicia also tended to overshadow her. Felicia seemed to seek a lot of attention and Udenka gave it to her in equal measure. They spent a whole day with them and it was time well spent. While they were there, they learnt that a film would be shown in the market square at night. They all agreed to meet up there at an agreed time and place.

A crowd had gathered by the time Udenka caught up with Felicia. The film was about to start, but she seemed restless and was hugging, kissing and cuddling at the same time. She demanded they leave the crowded arena for any isolated spot. It was pitch dark, so they were able to sneak out unnoticed. The film had now started and their disappearance seemed unnoticed. They walked along holding hands and she began to quicken her steps. They were fast advancing to an isolated building that stood on its own in the dark, and with his local knowledge, he knew it was unoccupied. They saw no human being nor heard any sound as they walked towards the building. She was breathing heavily, but as they got closer to the building the fear of being caught overwhelmed them and they beat a quick retreat. Felicia could not believe that having gone so far they were going back. Sadly, she could not have what she wanted so badly. It was in a village setting and there were no streets, never mind streetlights. It was pitch dark, dead quiet, and the little courage they had, initially propelled by a terrible urge, had suddenly deserted them. They quietly walked back holding hands, saying little before joining the crowd at the cinema.

The next morning, Udenka went with his friend to visit the two girls again. When they approached the house, they noticed a bicycle was parked by the side of the building. When they got inside, they met a man from a nearby village whom they knew. He was also a student. They spent several hours expecting the man to set off for home since he had quite a distance to cover, but he just wouldn't leave. He stayed and was so relaxed that Udenka and his friend left for their nearby homes. Both worked out a plan of going to the girls' place early in the morning the next day to get there before the cyclist from another village arrived. The following morning, they took off very early at 6 a.m. and to their consternation they sighted the bicycle already parked by the house. As if the cyclist knew the plan, he was there already. They had to turn back because it made no sense going in as the cyclist would outstay them. The whole process was repeated the next morning and again, the cyclist was there. They decided to stop going to the house and he never saw Felicia again. She eventually married a country's ruler.

Chapter Fifteen

Udenka's first day at medical school involved being taken round the various departments and introduced to their lecturers. For the students, it was an opportunity to meet each other. There were just a few girls in a class of thirty medical students. He did not fancy any of the girls. The visit that everyone was excited about was to the anatomy department. There they stood round a table, in the middle of which was placed a cadaver, and the lecturer started to demonstrate the various parts of the human body. Udenka was not moved by the strange and unusual sight. Ten minutes into the demonstration, one tall, slim male student in front of him suddenly started sweating and in the next few seconds he slumped to the floor, unconscious. He eventually recovered and was taken to the hostel. While discussing the incident with other students, Udenka tried to tell them there was no way the student who fainted would go on to become a doctor. He was so convinced that the boy was finished and would pursue another professional course rather than a medical degree. He was totally wrong. The next day, the student was calling the shots in the anatomy department as they began to dissect a cadaver allocated to them in a group of six students. He appeared very confident and unmoved by the exercise, even more in control than Udenka. First year was spent familiarising themselves with the various subjects they had to cover in the five years course.

He got busy in his second year because of a professional examination that would take place towards the end of the year. During lectures, he sat unnoticed at the back of the class and wrote using handwriting that only he could read, but he was able to take down the lecture, word for word. During a test on the subject, he reproduced the entire lecture to score full marks. The lecturers never noticed him as he remained almost invisible at the back, but when the results were released, the lecturers would be asking who he was.

There was a boy in their class who was a bit weird but clever. He would talk animatedly in class in between lectures, but as soon as a lecturer walked in and began to lecture, he instantly went to sleep, only to wake up as the teaching ended. At the end of the day, he would collect notes taken by other students. No effort was made to wake him up as it would be futile. He did not fail any examination, and he qualified as a doctor. He wouldn't stop dozing off in class all through his years at medical school. During ward rounds, this very student would sleep while standing, without swaying from side to side or ever keeling over. He was small and thin but really intelligent.

Udenka shared a bunk bed with his very close friend, Emeka, at the medical school hostel. He slept on top and Emeka slept below. They did everything together as they were so close to each other. Both worked hard in their studies and played games of football together. When eventually Emeka found a girlfriend and was spending more time with her, Udenka was devastated. Udenka was struggling to find a girlfriend but, at the same time, was able to stay concentrated on his studies. This paid off in the end as he was awarded a distinction in microbiology, along with his best friend. Both were nominated to go to the University of Rochester in the USA to study for a degree in microbiology. They were so pleased and excited to study abroad. In their excitement, they went to visit another student a year above them who dampened their joy and enthusiasm at going abroad. He told them they should calm down and obtain a medical degree first before anything else. They quietly retired to their hostel. The next day they turned the offer down.

Then came the first military coup, and then another, in quick succession. There was so much tension following the second coup that it became obvious things would not be the same again as tribal sentiments and divisions were so high. Events moved rapidly towards open conflict.

A civil war was fast approaching so Udenka had to go back to his tribal region, thereby interrupting his studies. He thought of staying out of the war at medical school but most of the students from his tribe were leaving, so he joined them.

The next three years were testing times. He first moved to stay with his mum and siblings in his village. He had only spent two years at medical school and was not yet exposed to the wards, so had no clinical experience to treat patients.

He decided with his classmates to meet in a specialist hospital in the township to see if a teaching programme could be organised for them. He stayed with a family friend, who was single, in a small rented room. He was much older than Udenka and had no job at the time, so he spent much time at home. He took Udenka with him whenever he went out as he was protecting his younger, pretty sister who was a student at a girls' school. She was on school holidays. His time with them was enjoyable. They made merry and caught up with old time stories. The family knew a lot of people in town and they spent most evenings visiting those they treasured.

Chapter Sixteen

Every day for two weeks, Udenka visited the hospital but nothing was being organised for them. He made up his mind that he was going back to the village. He decided to pay the hospital one last visit during an afternoon. While there, he heard a heavy sound, like a bomb or explosion.

People gathered and wondered what the sound could be. The civil war had started and was about two weeks old. One man in their midst volunteered to go the Governor's house to find out what was the source of the sound they heard. They waited and waited until he got back. On his return, he told them that it was a new weapon the government was testing. Eventually it turned out that the sound was coming from advancing enemy military forces heading towards the township. He travelled back to his village that very day and the town fell the next day.

To occupy his time, Udenka started going to a mission hospital about twenty miles away with a medical student from his homestead. His name was Okeke. Both decided to rent two separate rooms near the hospital rather than travel daily. It was a big hospital staffed by numerous trained and student nurses. The hospital was busy because there was no other hospital nearby. Both took part in ward rounds but did little if any clinical work. They travelled home on weekends usually together.

They were both students and had no source of income. Travelling up to the mission hospital was becoming too expensive and they could no longer afford it. They decided to settle in a small government hospital about two miles away from home. They were not allowed to touch patients or war-wounded in the hospital and were only required to sit in the clinic and wards observing doctors at work. It was during their period there that he came across a paragon of beauty who came to the hospital to visit a member of staff. She was a teenager who looked more like a model. She was tall, well-shaped, and her face was wonderfully attractive. She had a dreamy, romantic look. She was blessed with enviable good looks and was pleasantly well-mannered. She was elegantly well-dressed. Her gait was out of this world. She walked as if she floated, her feet touching the ground gently without a sound, even on a hard surface. She was visiting him often at the hospital and they got on well. She had a good sense of humour and was fond of cracking childish but funny jokes. She was so feminine, as demonstrated by her looks, the way she walked, and the sweet sound of her voice. Udenka felt that finally he had found the love of his life. Their relationship was short-lived unfortunately but joyous. She came to the hospital one morning and, from her looks, Udenka knew there was a problem. They sat down on a bench outside the hospital ward, and she explained that while she was in a busy open market three days previously in her village, a rich village chief and businessman with plenty of money to throw about saw her momentarily and was consumed by her looks. He proposed to her there and then and without delay took her to meet her mother. According to her, when they got there, the man threw money about so much so that the family went numb and gave the poor girl away. Even though he was rich, there was an obvious age gap. She told Udenka that her mother was happy with the relationship because of the money being bandied around.

Udenka asked her what she wanted. She told him she would go ahead with the marriage/relationship because of the poor financial situation of her mum and family. Both sat there speechless and cried. Udenka could not be consoled. They parted and moved on. The very wonderful and smooth relationship they enjoyed suddenly was brought to an end by the chance meeting in the market square of his girlfriend and the businessman.

Chapter Seventeen

The civil war was at its height and Udenka's people began to lose territories. The enemy soldiers were advancing. Soon the villagers began to hear the sound of armoured cars and heavy tanks. Two days prior to this, Udenka began to regret not staying behind at the medical school and thought that the decision to come home was the wrong one. It pained him that the war had interrupted his medical course. The night before they evacuated, his parent and siblings were busy packing and hiding important documents in a pit dug overnight. Udenka pretended to go along with this preparation to move out to a safer town. He had decided on that last night that he wasn't going to move but would rather be captured by enemy soldiers who would then take him back to medical school to continue with his interrupted medical studies. He told no family members about this plan of his. The next morning, they packed up and took whatever they could carry with them and the entire family departed. Udenka pretended to move out with them and then made a beeline for the house they had just evacuated, unnoticed. He got back to his room and waited to be captured. As he crouched under the bed, he could hear the approaching armoured vehicles. The parent and siblings totalled eleven without him so in the heat of the moment, it went unnoticed that he was missing. They had covered two miles before it was noticed that Udenka was surprisingly not in their midst. His brave brother, Ignatius, who worked for an oil company, volunteered to return to the house to search for Udenka. Time was of the essence because of the rapidly advancing enemy. Ignatius was brave, strong and bold. He had to run fast back to the house, straight to Udenka's room, to find him hiding under the bed. He manhandled him, shouting at him at the same time. He was forcibly pushed and both rushed out of the house. By this time, bullets from armoured vehicles were already falling in front of the house and they had to run away crouching and crawling. It was a close call. Udenka was naïve in thinking that if captured by the enemy soldiers they would have spared him and sent him back to continue with his education.

They walked for days, moving from one town to another, until they settled in a town seventy miles from home. Initially, he was unable to locate where his fellow medical student, Okeke, and housemate had moved to but eventually, news slowly filtered in about his whereabouts and location. He moved quickly to join him at a small mission hospital close to the war front. The hospital was run by Irish nuns who provided the two with accommodation. The nuns also prepared wonderful meals for them including breakfast and sumptuous lunches. There were nurses in training and the rules were very strict; the nurses feared the nuns so much that they were too afraid to talk to the two medical students. Apart from the wonderful meals and care provided to them, the two found it tough going, as they were unable to forge any form of relationship with the girls around them because of disciplinary actions that could be applied to the trainee nurses. The situation remained like that for about a couple of months, but they kept busy in the hospital helping war-wounded and sick civilians.

He became attached to one of the surgeons in the hospital, who had a girlfriend who was the daughter of a college principal known for his strictness. She was living with this surgeon friend. One day, her younger sister visited her and after a time, she tried to shake her sister off but when she couldn't she called Udenka and introduced her to him. She took him aside and warned him that her younger sister was strange and difficult at most times and not easy to handle. Following the introduction, he took her younger sister to his room where they spent a couple of hours together. It was a quiet day for him as he was not working and he hoped to have a good time. It has been six months since the arrival of Udenka and Okeke at the mission hospital, and they were yet to find girls to befriend due to the stricture imposed on the nursing staff.

The war went on and on, unabated, and Udenka and Okeke remained at the same hospital. They progressively got busy at the hospital as an increasing number of war-wounded continued to arrive. The two had not made any progress in finding girlfriends. They were making efforts, but nothing seemed to work.

There was a student nurse, Kate, whom everyone in the town talked about in superlative terms – what she looked like and why she was adored by all. Kate was endowed with natural beauty, and her student nurse colleagues were in awe of her as she was overbearing and intimidating. She had a tall, slim boyfriend who was so proud of what he had that he regarded others with contempt. He was annoyingly pompous and felt he was so knowledgeable and that he knew more than others. He had no patience with the downtrodden and disadvantaged. Udenka was prepared for him as he was already well briefed about him by the people who had fallen out with him. One time, he made the mistake of challenging Udenka while with this very special nurse whom everyone indulged in talking about; Udenka disgracefully rubbished him. He was dumbfounded and unable to respond like a man. His girlfriend, who regarded him as brave and courageous, was taken aback.

Three days later, he was approaching a corridor in a poorly lit area of the hospital when Kate suddenly appeared from nowhere. She had an aggressive walk as if about to challenge someone to a fight. There was no grace in her movements and you could hear her steps half a mile away. She stamped the ground hard. She was majestic as she approached but at the same time muscular and certainly had physical presence. There was something about her that was intimidating and it was nothing more than her beauty. Her appearance and presence would disarm a weak soul. Kate was light in complexion and not very fluent in English and as such, spoke little English, preferring to talk in native dialect. They spoke to each other briefly and she agreed to meet him again. Udenka was happy and surprised at her acceptance of a further meeting because she was so close to her boyfriend that everyone knew they were to marry. At their second meeting, they got on so well that she decided to drop her proud boyfriend. She was in such demand that she had an army officer she told Udenka about. Kate told him whenever she would visit the army officer and normally spent three days with him. She was quite open about it and never hid it from him.

With her light complexion, she had a lovely, well-developed body. Her thighs were smooth and supple. She visited most evenings when the nuns had retired to the convent. Because of all the restrictions on their movements, her evening visits were short.

Chapter Eighteen

Udenka was eventually moved to a small community hospital that was devoted to treating mainly injured soldiers. Sick villagers were also allowed to come for treatment. He lived in a caravan located in an open space within the hospital grounds. The hospital originally served as a mission hospital serving a thinly populated town before the civil war. He helped to run clinics. The hospital was situated in an open ground unshielded by trees and was often subjected to bombing from the air. There was a bank nearby and bank workers often came for treatment.

One morning, at about ten o'clock, he was in one of the consulting rooms helping to see a young girl who had come from the nearby bank for treatment. She was well known in the community and well regarded for her pleasantness and good manners. Udenka also knew her as she was very helpful to him each time he was at the bank to withdraw money. That morning, she ended up in the consulting room where Udenka was. She arrived from the bank having been taken ill suddenly. As she lay on the couch to be examined, two fighter jets came swooping in without warning and started bombing the hospital. Anyone fit enough ran for cover. There was nothing else but to run for cover. Udenka dived under the couch while the hospital was continuously strafed. It lasted for about seven minutes. When the jet fighters disappeared, Udenka crawled out from under the couch only to discover the bank worker dead on the couch, killed by the air raid. Udenka held her hand as no one was around and cried loudly leaning over her. He just continued to hold her hand tightly. News of her death spread so quickly as she was well known. Her bank colleagues came rushing in, and when they saw the lifeless body on the couch, they fell to the ground and wept and wept endlessly. Udenka could not take it any longer. He wished he was rather dead. He quickly retired to his caravan which by now had several bullet holes and cried himself to sleep like a child as no one could console him for he lived alone.

As the civil war intensified, so did the bombing. There was a rumour spreading among the doctors that interested Udenka; for him at least it was a badly needed form of diversion, away from the atrocities he was witnessing first-hand. He recently heard a gossip about a young couple he seemed not to know. They lived over fifty miles away in a field hospital. He heard about them from different sources. In a nutshell, it was said that the man's wife was weird, smallish and very short-tempered. Her husband was a doctor. It was said that his wife often slapped him in public at the slightest provocation. If true, this story would be regarded as an abomination. Udenka could not comprehend it. He doubted the story. How could it happen? His people adhered strictly to native law and customs where it was unheard of that a woman would strike a man first, not to mention it being witnessed by others. Because he had strong doubts about what he was hearing, the informants advised him to pay a visit to the couple. One morning, he set off with a companion who knew them. They travelled walking and using public transport and halfway into the journey they were getting close to a big open market. As they got closer, they heard the frightening sound of fighter jets, about two in number, hovering so low that they had to dash into the bush to take cover. They flew past so low that they could see the pilots. The fighter jets soon flew past and started bombing a target nearby. They could not make out the target from where they were. There was a market nearby that occupied a large expanse of land and served several villages and towns. They could tell from the noise that something was amiss. When they eventually arrived at the market to see the carnage before them, it became clear that the market was the site of the bombing. It was so visible and unobscured that it could easily be identified from the sky as a market and nothing else as such to write home about.

The crying, wailing and grieving would remain etched in his memory. Both spent hours in the market place attending the wounded and providing support to the bereaved. The scene was unimaginable.

With a heavy heart, Udenka continued in trying to complete the remaining part of this meaningless journey with his companion. When they eventually arrived at the house, they found the couple standing outside in front of the building talking to a male guest. He was introduced to the couple. They continued to chat outside, moving from one topic to the other. Eventually, the discussion shifted to a new subject. The atmosphere was genial and everyone felt comfortable and free to butt in. The doctor, on trying to contribute to the discussion, having seemed subdued for a time, said something innocuous. The wife suddenly became irritated and within a split second of her husband closing his mouth, she jumped up and landed a big slap on her husband's face. It was so dramatic. Udenka was taken aback. He rubbed both eyes to make sure he was seeing correctly. Udenka was stunned; his legs felt wooden and remained rooted on the ground. He could not move for a considerable length of time. When he eventually pulled himself together, he walked off with his friend saying nothing.

The war that appeared never to end suddenly came to a stop. Udenka caught up with his mother and the rest of the siblings and they began to gather their belongings for the return journey home. As they set off, Udenka's girlfriend, Kate, appeared suddenly, having covered sixty miles to join him. Udenka was so surprised at the coincidence, how she just arrived as they were leaving. They travelled along and at some point Udenka and Kate separated from his mother and siblings in order to feel free. They ended up at his cousin's house. His cousin was single but had loads of male friends who were temporarily visiting. Udenka asked him if he could house them. He refused bluntly and Udenka was devastated. That wicked refusal was to change the life of Kate forever. They left the house immediately and had nowhere to go but to join the rest of his family with her in tow. The entourage eventually settled in a house in a little town they arrived at after a day's journey. The atmosphere in the house was a bit tense and Kate rightly did not feel welcomed enough. She felt that the treatment was stifling her. Udenka was observing it all and could not understand it. She was being looked at times as if she had committed a crime. She was basically nothing more than a girlfriend to a family member. It was a difficult time for Udenka and Kate. The situation both found themselves in was to impact on Kate's life forever. It was a very dangerous time because women and girls were been whisked away. That kind of behaviour was out of control. It was all in the news. Kate was hinting at leaving, but Udenka told her it was too dangerous. He was a student and had no money to rent a flat.

Godwin noticed that all was not well and told Udenka his plan of getting a flat nearby the next day for him and Kate. The very next morning, Kate had decided she was leaving. Both were engaged in discussions. It was a deeply emotional morning. Udenka tried to convince her that it was not safe at all as he saw the previous day uniformed men picking up people in the market square like toys. She was hell-bent on leaving. With a heavy heart, he escorted her to the road where she joined a vehicle going to her hospital and not her hometown. She got there safely but on reaching there and seeing her female colleagues hiding as it was not safe to venture out, she began to worry about her parents' safety at home. She was so attached to them. Her father loved her so much. She became restless again and threw caution to the wind, deciding to make another dangerous journey home. Her luck ran out.

Chapter Nineteen

It took Udenka and his family three days to reach their hometown, only to discover that their house was no more, flattened by the fighting. The treasure buried in the compound had been dug up and taken, including valuable family pictures. They moved to a rented house and began to count the pieces. Udenka was in a hurry to get back to medical school after three years of war during which his classmates, not at all affected by the civil war, were in the final year and about to qualify as doctors. There was no money to travel back to the medical school – two hundred miles away. He decided to travel to the township close to the local airport. The next morning, he walked for seven miles to the airport, hoping to fly to the capital where the medical school was situated, without a ticket. There was no money to buy one. He spent a whole day at the airport and there was no flight. He went to the airport every day for seven days but could not travel. Then one day, he was at the airport when suddenly, at lunchtime, a large military plane landed. When the plane was about to depart there was an announcement asking for people who wanted to travel to the capital to join the flight. He jumped up, excited, and began to walk down to the aircraft when a man who knew his older brother pulled him back and asked him what he was trying to do. Udenka told him his plight, how he had spent several days at the airport. He explained to Udenka that there was no insurance to cover him in case the plane crashed as it was a military aircraft. He listened and took his advice and walked back to town in despair. Days later his brother, Godwin, managed to raise enough money and he travelled by road back to school.

When he got back to the medical school, he was well supported by the schoolmates he had left three years previously. It was hard times because there was no money in part caused by not winning the war. He worked hard as he did not want to lose more years. His classmates unaffected by the war were in their final year. Those in his class affected by the war, like himself, were worried stiff about parents and siblings left at home, struggling to survive under an unimaginable situation, brought upon them by losing the civil war. He kept his head down studying and attending lectures, hoping nothing would distract him. Kate eventually visited Udenka in the medical school and both chatted so much about the civil war and what happened when it came to an end. They were very careful to avoid things that should never be discussed. Kate spent just one night at his hostel. She was in a difficult situation and needed emotional and all sorts of help as she was going through a lot and her last hope in life was Udenka. At that juncture when Udenka should stand firm with her, he did not feel for her. He reminded her of what happened when he paid her the only visit in the hospital where she worked, she was not seen even though he slept in her room. She never came back that night to stay with him. It was her housemate that kept him company until he went to bed that night. They decided to part because of that incident that hurt Udenka badly. She was devastated. With a heavy heart, he parted ways with her.

The courses became more interesting when Udenka started going to the wards of the teaching hospital and seeing clinical cases first-hand. More importantly, he liked to watch clinicians examine patients and see the way in which they arrived at a diagnosis. He spent more time on the wards hoping that by doing so, rare cases might turn up. He was rewarded two weeks later when, having spent nearly ten hours in the Accident and Emergency department, a man with rabies arrived. The news spread so fast that doctors, medical students and hospital staff were rushing to witness it first-hand for the first time. Within a short space of time, the department was crowded. Many watched from a distance and were distressed by the sound coming from the afflicted man. Among the doctors who rushed to see the case of something they had read about in textbooks but had never seen in person was a young specialist physician who had just returned from the United Kingdom, where he had trained. He brought back with him a large black Alsatian. He was so moved by what he saw and was overwhelmed with fear that he rushed home, picked up his gun and shot his Alsatian dead.

His course was progressing well and he moved from one specialty to another including medicine, surgery, public health, psychiatry, paediatrics, and obstetrics and gynaecology. He found obstetrics more daunting. He spent time in the labour wards observing midwives delivering babies until it came to his turn to do the same. The first baby he delivered really excited him and he told the story for weeks, even though he had little to do with it. It was the midwife who did most of the work and his input was minimal. Yet when he told the tale, he said he was alone in the cubicle and delivered the baby unassisted. As he boasted to his colleagues in training, they were in awe of him for undertaking the task all on his own.

Time moved so quickly for him. He could not believe how far he had gone in the course.

He was now in his final year and he knew it was going to be busy. He hoped there would be no distraction. There was nothing really to distract him. He was about the only final-year medical student without a girlfriend. He couldn't find one. His last effort fizzled out. This was what happened. He met a student nurse working in the same ward of the teaching hospital and they began to talk to each other for a couple of weeks. It seemed to be working and he felt it was almost cemented. They agreed to attend a party together. The party was held yearly outside the hospital and was normally well attended. On the appointed evening, Udenka dressed quickly as the time for the scheduled pick up of his new girl was fast approaching and he didn't want to be late in picking up his first date. He wore a trendy suit and nicely polished black pointed shoes that he had borrowed. He then walked to the nurses' hostel where she lived. When he got there and asked for her, she was nowhere to be found. He was told by another girl at the hostel that the girl had gone to the same party with an unidentified male. Udenka found it strange that she could have gone without him. It was a solid arrangement made of stone. He concluded that for her to behave the way she did meant she must be heartless. He went back to his accommodation in a bad state. He least expected what had happened, more so because she gave him firm assurance she would partner him to the party. He could not comprehend it. He undressed and went straight to bed and slept poorly that night. He kept on turning in bed and sighing at the same time.

There was an event Udenka had to attend two hundred miles away, six months before his final examination. His brother, Godwin, was about to wed and he travelled to the town where his brother lived, where the ceremony would take place in a matter of days. Godwin was staying temporarily in a government reserved area of the town in a spacious bungalow. Udenka travelled overnight and arrived there in the morning to be greeted by his brother's young wife and four girls from her school of similar age. She introduced him to her girlfriends who were excited to meet an equally young handsome man, particularly a medical student living and studying in the capital of the country. There was a buzz about provincial girls meeting anyone who happened to live in the capital. All morning they swarmed round him asking questions relating to life in the capital.

The boldest of the girls, Grace by name, quickly declared an interest in Udenka and began to intimidate and ward off the other girls. The girls were also equally interested in him and it became obvious that the boldest would succeed. Grace was plump, tall, and bigger than all the other girls. She had a big, commanding voice, was aggressive in nature, and seemed the boldest of the group. She was not as beautiful as the rest of the girls. The struggle for him spilled over and his brother's wife intervened with a warning. She warned Udenka to be extremely careful with her friends and that he should just concentrate on the wedding, after which he should hurry back to the capital to complete his studies. She was wary of one of the girls, the one who imposed herself on Udenka. The struggle fizzled out. The other girls cooled off and kept their distance but knew what would befall him. Grace was all over him throughout the day. She seemed to be so much in love, kissing and holding hands, hugging and touching. He had no choice but to go along. She was not as beautiful as the rest of his friends.

That same day, in the evening, they dressed for the bachelor's eve to be held in the town hall. They travelled together to the big hall at about seven o'clock in the evening. At the time, guests were initially trickling in, but it became crowded within an hour. They all sat down on long benches while the music played loudly. Grace never gave him any breathing space to talk to her schoolmates who had come with them, and they were equally intimidated and fearful of her because they knew she was aggressive. They watched the two from a distance to see how things played out. A lot of boys came without partners and gradually began to chat up the girls.

The bachelor, Godwin, arrived and opened the dance floor and people began to dance to the music. The dance floor was full and people kept dancing and having a wonderful time. Udenka and Grace were together most of the time. She kept him within sight, so that he was unable to dance with the three other girls they came with. The crowd made merry until around midnight when a well-known local television personality, entertainer and dancer suddenly arrived from nowhere. Within thirty minutes of him arriving, there was a total blackout in the hall. At the time, Grace was on the dance floor and Udenka was outside, being introduced to the daughter of a very rich man from his town. When the lights came back on five minutes later, Grace was nowhere to be seen. She had disappeared into thin air. Someone, probably the latecomer had created the blackout and escaped with her. Udenka found himself suddenly alone, without a partner. The other girls he came with had picked partners at the venue and showed little sympathy for him. They saw it coming. He went back to the house alone. The next day the girls were returning one by one to get ready for the wedding scheduled for the afternoon. Of course, Grace was yet to return. She was the chief bridesmaid but was late for the wedding. The other girls did not want to have anything to do with him for failing to realise what a bad choice he had made in choosing such a character.

Chapter Twenty

He travelled back the next day after the wedding, knowing he had only six months before he graduated from medical school. He knew he had to work hard and be well prepared for his final examination. He kept busy so it was with reluctance that he accepted a lunch invitation from a couple from his town who were now living in the same city where he was studying. Despite being busy, he looked forward to the lunch date and made sure he wouldn't forget the day. On previous occasions, they were known to provide sumptuous meals and not the rubbish meals he was used to at medical school. When he got to the couple's home, he met other guests also invited to lunch, among them a girl in her twenties who had come alone. She appeared to be elegant, eloquent and knowledgeable. She was well turned out and spoke in a soft voice. Udenka envied her accent and command of the English language. As he listened to the conversation going on around him, it seemed she would have spent some time in Europe.

When lunch was ready, they were ushered to the dining table and seated. The main dish was chicken soup and pounded yam. Apart from the hostess, there was only this girl who sat down surrounded by men in the dining area. They totalled eight in number. The lone girl was the first one allowed to take soup from the soup plate with a big spoon. When she had finished taking the soup, the bowl was passed round. Udenka was so hungry, as he hadn't eaten all day on purpose to arrive with an empty stomach. He waited patiently for his turn to come. Suddenly, an argument started slowly between the seated men and the polished girl sitting opposite Udenka, which then reached feverish pitch. He soon realised the source of the dispute. The westernised girl had put the only gizzard in the soup into her soup plate, and she was told by the male guests that it was wrong and very disrespectful to the men around her to behave that way. It was unheard of and an abomination for her to take what was traditionally meant only for male folks. She blatantly refused to do that and really stood her ground. She would not be intimidated. She was not in the least prepared to back down. There was obviously a stalemate. The men quickly got up and left the house. The girl soon departed saying nothing to the host and hostess, unrepentant at leaving all the cooked food uneaten. Udenka went back to the medical school hungry, miserable and dejected. He wondered what all these traditional beliefs were all about. He bought a loaf of bread on his way back and that was all he had to eat because by the time he got back, lunch was no longer served and the dining room was locked at that time.

Eventually, his class sat the final examination, which stretched for over two weeks and included written and oral tests. The whole process was intensive. It had taken five years at medical school to get to that point in time – an unenviable feat. The worst torture was to come: the anxious wait for the examination results. He could hardly sleep. The mistakes he made in his weak subjects came flooding in, magnified in his dream state, whenever he managed to sleep. He lacked appetite and he had become more irritable to the point of avoiding his classmates. To make his current situation more depressing, he soon remembered that he had spent five years at the institution and was almost the only one in his class who had failed to find a girlfriend. This very failing began to haunt him.

When the results were released, he was glad to have passed. His joy was cut short when he realised that his friend had not made it, having failed in his subjects. His joy was tinged with sadness particularly so because his friend took his failure very badly. A week later, his mates organised a leaving party, which he had to attend. There was so much going on at the party and alcohol was flowing freely. He soon realised a few friends wanted him drunk by all means because of their keenness in topping up his glass with strong alcohol. To survive he mastered a plan. Each time they filled his glass and went back to the dance floor, he would sneak into the toilet and empty the glass into the sink only to have it refilled by them as soon as he returned. At the end of the party, he was the only one standing; the rest were dead stoned.

Eventually, he moved to the eastern part of the country to be closer to his siblings, even though he was given a job in the teaching hospital where he trained. There he found a job in a specialist hospital. Initially, he lived on the university campus for a while. He was advised not to leave any personal belongings when going out but to take everything with him otherwise nothing would be left when he got back. He settled well into the job and began to make friends in abundance. He had no problems in finding girls, as he did during medical school. He hoped to progress in his career by working hard and showing interest in his medical profession. Now that he was practising as a medical doctor, he felt satisfied with his job and was happy in choosing to do medicine rather than chemistry for which he was offered a place. Udenka remembered how a close friend of his came from his university to visit him in the medical school a distance of fifty miles. This friend came all the way only to tell him off for not accepting to do chemistry in a top university to which he belonged. Udenka was very surprised he came all the way for that but said nothing. His friend even told him bluntly that the medical school was nothing to compare to the top university he had turned down.

He gradually progressed in his new but admirable profession. He became more confident in accepting more clinical responsibilities. Long hours of work and been on call at night did not create any problem for him. He closely observed more senior colleagues in order to develop good clinical skills.

Six months later, he had to attend a conference nearer his hometown. He booked into a hotel that was newly opened in a quiet part of town. It was a Friday evening. He checked in and was told there was a party going on by the hotel pool. He was also informed there was a live band playing. When he got to his hotel room, he rang a distant cousin, Vivian, to join him at the poolside. At the pool, he sat alone on a chair next to a table that seated three people. Soon, Vivian arrived and trailing behind her was another girl. He did not know she was coming with someone else. It was a surprise. Following a brief conversation, they settled down to eat and drink, at the same time soaking up the lively music emanating from the live band on stage at the other side of the pool. The vocalist was singing native songs and now moving closer to where Udenka sat. He was busy sipping red wine while the two girls ate and drank fruit cocktail. The new girl said little. She was not particularly pretty, but Udenka felt there was something special about her. She was adorned with well-cropped hair of a rare nice colour. When she got up to visit the Ladies, she seemed tender and feminine. She walked delicately and tenderly, as if afraid to walk. She had a well-shaped backside that made her well rounded and attractive.

As the night wore thin, the music became more pleasurable. The vocalist was now next to him singing at the top of his voice. Udenka put his hand in his pocket and money exchanged hands. At the poolside, there was a photographer. The two girls who sat next to him were busy taking pictures. From time to time, they would ask him to join. When the vocalist got back on the stage, the drummer was next to descend on Udenka. The music went on and on so that by the time the party was coming to an end everyone there was satisfied . Exhausted band members stopped playing suddenly. At that point, Udenka retired with the two girls to his hotel room in the early hours of the morning. In the room, the new girl sat on the cushion while Udenka lay on the bed busily thinking of the best way to approach her. It was more difficult because she had said very little all night. Vivian sat down on a chair and was busy reading a novel placed on a table next to the bathroom. Eventually, he summoned enough courage to ask the taciturn girl to join him in bed. To his surprise, she willingly did as she was asked. She came close to him in bed and was easy-going, touching and holding him. Her skin was smooth, warm and soft to the touch. She was fair in complexion and loved being touched and caressed.

She now opened up and they chatted for some time. She spoke easily and told him that she hadn't seen her former boyfriend and was missing him.

She thought that he might have gone abroad and made no further contact. She was quite young, pleasant and nice. He warmed to her and enjoyed stroking her tender, smooth skin. When it became obvious that she would go far with him, he got up and went to Vivian, sitting by the table still pretending to read her novel, but it appeared she was listening to the conversation going on in the room. The light in the room was still on. Udenka begged her to retire to the bathroom to continue with her novel but she refused to move, despite his vehemently beseeching her in no uncertain terms. Udenka always knew her as a strange girl. He even shouted at her and threatened her. Vivian ignored him and stayed put. He was by now very aggravated and not knowing what to do next, he went back and moved closer to the girl with the nicely coloured hair. Vivian now dramatically advanced towards them, with her novel held in one hand. She sat on a cushion placed parallel and very close to the bed watching the two. By now, the new girl started to cry over her lost boyfriend. It was a cry of sadness rather than cry of joy. It was a loud, purposeful weeping outside her control. It was loud enough that Vivian now seemed rattled and her head rotated towards her friend now crying so much.

Suddenly, Vivian got up, now very worked up and more agitated with her eyes bulging. She was asking the new girl aggressively and repeatedly why she was crying so much. She was saying over and over again to her, "Why are you crying, why are you crying, why are you crying?" She now came much closer. Udenka's anger began to build up more and more. The question was being repeated because Vivian wanted an answer. Having moved closer to them now, Vivian leaned over the bed and came face to face with her friend and kept on asking her to tell her why she was crying. Vivian was worried stiff that something was wrong with her friend. When Vivian came so close, Udenka felt it was time to call it off.

He ran into the bathroom upset with Vivian and wished her dead for refusing to obey him when asked to move into the bathroom. The crying seized soon after and Vivian went back to her chair and continued with her novel. Immediately, in the bathroom, the crying of the girl with the strange hair brought back to Udenka a long-forgotten childhood memory, the crying of the parents who lost a child during a bee chase that he was involved in. He lost his composure and started to shed tears. He could now hear the wailing and screaming and the sound of chasing bees. It once more came to haunt him, an event in his childhood that he assumed he had forgotten for good. He could not escape from it.

Bibliography

John Anakwenze was born in Okwe, Nigeria in early forties. His father, a head teacher, died when John was very young. He struggled badly in the early part of his education but eventually won a scholarship to read medicine in the College of Medicine, University of Lagos, Nigeria. His medical training was interrupted by the Nigerian civil war. He qualified as a doctor in 1973. He was employed as a junior doctor in Enugu Specialist Hospital, Nigeria from 1973–1976 before leaving for United Kingdom for postgraduate studies on East Central State Government scholarship. He arrived back to Nigeria in 1985 and lectured in Nuclear Medicine in University of Nigeria Teaching Hospital from 1985-1990. In 1990 he moved back to United Kingdom. He is currently working in NHS hospitals as a Locum Consultant Physician in Geriatric Medicine. He is married with seven children.

One Page Synopsis

This is a nonfiction narrative. The main character is Udenka. The story takes off in the early forties when he was four years old. He struggled to get into a primary school due to his small stature and describes early in his life what life was like in the village in those days.

While at home alone with his younger sister, an eclipse of the sun occurred around the end of the Second World War and Udenka observed the reaction of the villagers.

When he was eventually accepted into the primary school, an event took place in which he was chased by angry bees along with his peers and he made a narrow escape. The chase ended in a fatality and he was very shaken by the event and he stopped schooling temporarily.

He moved to the township to live with his elder brother, Godwin. He got exposed to life in the township and the decadence. His concentration at studies took a tumble and he was expelled.

He was recalled by his parents where he resumed schooling. His father, Fidelis, was a head teacher and courageous man. Fidelis failed Udenka when his courage was tested – he could not kill a snake. Unfortunately, Fidelis took suddenly ill and died leaving behind a young wife and ten children. For Udenka and his siblings, it was a time of immense suffering. A Good Samaritan arrived and picked Udenka to live with her in a college where she was newly employed to teach. There, Udenka started secondary school. When she left for the university a year later, Udenka had to change to another school to complete '0' level course. Luckily he passed the entrance examination into a government college for 'A' level science course. He then moved to a medical school to read medicine. His studies were interrupted by the civil war and he described his experience during the civil war. He eventually qualified as a doctor.

His efforts to find a girlfriend make interesting reading and impacted on the story. It describes vividly how he was let down several times by people he trusted.

The last paragraph of the narrative illustrates how an event (The Bee Chase) he thought he had completely forgotten surfaced suddenly and showed that the trauma /experience was there to stay. He could not escape from it. It was still very raw.

Dedication

FOR

Mr. Fidelis Anakwenze

AND

Mrs. Udego Anakwenze
My parents,
May they Rest in peace

HERZ FÜR AUTOREN A HEART FOR AUTHORS À L'ÉCOUTE DES AUTEURS MIA ΚΑΡΔΙΑ ΓΙΑ ΣΥ
RITA FÖR FÖRFATTARE UN CORAZÓN POR LOS AUTORES YAZARLARIMIZA GÖNÜL VERELIM
ORE PER AUTORI ET HJERTE FOR FORFATTERE EEN HART VOOR SCHRIJVERS TEMOS OS AU
ZÖINKÉRT SERCE DLA AUTORÓW EIN HERZ FÜR AUTOREN A HEART FOR AUTHORS À L'ÉC
ΡΑÇÃO ВСЕЙ ДУШОЙ К АВТОРАМ ETT HJÄRTA FÖR FÖRFATTARE À LA ESCUCHA DE LOS AU
EURS MIA ΚΑΡΔΙΑ ΓΙΑ ΣΥΓΓΡΑΦΕΙΣ UN CUORE PER AUTORI ET HJERTE FOR FORFATTERE EE
ARIMIZA GÖ   RE   ZÖINKÉRT SERCE DLA AUTORÓW EIN HERZ F
R SCHRIJVERS   S C   ÇÃO ВСЕЙ ДУШОЙ К АВТОРАМ ETT HJÄRTA

The author

Dr. John Anakwenze was born in Okwe, Nigeria in
the early forties. His father, a head teacher, died
when John was very young. He struggled badly in
the early part of his education but eventually won
a scholarship to study medicine in the College of
Medicine at the University of Lagos in Nigeria. His
medical training was interrupted by the Nigerian
Civil War. He qualified as a doctor in 1973 and was
employed as a junior doctor in Enugu Specialist
Hospital, Nigeria from 1973–1976 before going
to United Kingdom for postgraduate studies
on East Central State Government Scholarship.
He went back to Nigeria in 1985 and lectured
in Nuclear Medicine at the University of Nigeria
teaching hospital from 1985–1990. In 1990, John
moved back to the UK. He is currently working in
NHS Hospitals as a Locum Consultant Physician
in Geriatric Medicine. He is married with seven
children and enjoys reading and traveling in his
spare time.

novum PUBLISHER FOR NEW AUTHORS

The publisher

He who stops getting better stops being good.

This is the motto of novum publishing, and our focus is on finding new manuscripts, publishing them and offering long-term support to the authors.
Our publishing house was founded in 1997, and since then it has become THE expert for new authors and has won numerous awards.

Our editorial team will peruse each manuscript within a few weeks free of charge and without obligation.

You will find more information about
novum publishing and our books on the internet:

w w w . n o v u m - p u b l i s h i n g . c o . u k